WONDERDADS

THE BEST DAD/CHILD ACTIVITIES IN ST. LOUIS

CONTACT WONDERDADS

WonderDads books may be purchased for educational and promotional use. For information, please email us at store@wonderdads.com.

If you are interested in partnership opportunities with WonderDads, please email us at partner@wonderdads.com.

If you are interested in selling WonderDads books and other products in your region, please email us at hiring@wonderdads.com.

For corrections, recommendations on what to include in future versions of the book, updates or any other information, please email us at info@wonderdads.com.

©2011 WonderDads, Inc.
Book Authored by Adam Bodendieck & the WonderDads Staff
Cover & Book design by Crystal Langley. Proofread by Amy Harding & the WonderDads Staff.
All rights reserved. Printed in the United States of America.
No part of this publication may be reproduced or distributed in any form or by any means, or stored in a database or retrieval system, except as permitted under Sections 107 or 108 of the U.S. Copyright Act, without prior written permission of the publisher. This book is printed on acid-free paper.
Activities in this book should only be done with adult supervision. WonderDads encourages parents to not engage in any activities they feel could be harmful to their child or that their child may try to do again without an adult presence. WonderDads assumes no liability for any direct or indirect injuries that occur when using this book.

ISBN: 978-1-935153-45-0
First Printing, 2011
10 9 8 7 6 5 4 3 2 1

WONDERDADS ST. LOUIS
Table of Contents

pg. **9**
The Best of St. Louis

pg. **13**
The Best Dad/Child Restaurants

pg. **27**
The Best Dad/Child Activities

pg. **49**
The Best Dad/Child Stores

pg. **79**
The Best Dad/Child Outdoor Parks & Recreation

pg. **95**
The Best Dad/Child Sporting Events

pg. **103**
The Best Dad/Child Unique Adventures

FREE ACCESS FOR ONE YEAR ON YOUR SMARTPHONE!

Content From this Book, Special Updates & More on your

IPHONE, BLACKBERRY OR ANDROID

Take 10 Seconds to Register at
www.WonderDads.com/mobile.asp

We'll Then Email You the Special
Web Address and Your Username/Password

WELCOME TO WONDERDADS ST. LOUIS

Like so many other Dads, I love being with my kids, but struggle to find the right work/home balance. We are a part of a generation where Dads play much more of an active role with their kids, yet the professional and financial strains are greater than ever. We hope that the ideas in this book make it a little easier to be inspired to do something that makes you a hero in the eyes of your children.

This part of our children's lives goes by too fast, but the memories from a WonderDads inspired trip, event, meal, or activity last a long time (and will probably be laughed about when they grow up). So plan a Daddy day once a week, make breakfast together every Saturday morning, watch your football team every Sunday, or whatever works for you, and be amazed how long they will remember the memories and how good you will feel about yourself in the process.

Our warmest welcome to WonderDads.

Sincerely,

Jonathan Aspatore, **Founder & Dad**
Charlie (4) and Luke (3)

THE TOP 10 OVERALL BEST DAD/CHILD THINGS TO DO

Cardinals Baseball Game . . . . pg. 99

Chesterfield Sports Fusion . . . . pg. 46

Circus Flora . . . . pg. 32

City Museum . . . . pg. 28

Geocaching . . . . pg. 106

Grant's Farm . . . . pg. 42

The Great Forest Park Balloon Race . . . . pg. 81

St. Louis Science Center and OMNIMAX Theater . . . pg. 31

St. Louis Zoo . . . . pg. 31

Ted Drewes Concrete and Christmas Tree Lot . . . . . pg. 41

TOP 5 DAD/CHILD RESTAURANTS

City Diner	pg. 16
Fitz's Rootbeer	pg. 23
Forest Park Boathouse	pg. 15
Incredible Pizza Company	pg. 19
Luvy Duvy's Café	pg. 20

TOP 5 DAD/CHILD ACTIVITIES

City Museum	pg. 28
Gateway Arch and Museum of Westward Expansion	pg. 28
Home Depot Kids Workshop	pg. 34
Magic House	pg. 34
St. Louis Zoo	pg. 31

TOP 5 DAD/CHILD OUTDOOR PARKS & RECREATION

City Garden	pg. 80
Forest Park	pg. 81
Lafayette Park	pg. 87
Lone Elk Park	pg. 91
Turtle Playground	pg. 82

TOP 5 DAD/CHILD THINGS TO DO ON A RAINY DAY

Archiver's	pg. 73
Crown Candy Kitchen	pg. 14
Dave and Buster's	pg. 18
Flamingo Bowl	pg. 28
Moolah Theater and Lounge	pg. 33

TOP 5 DAD/CHILD THINGS TO DO ON A HOT DAY

Boathouse in Forest Park .... pg. 30
Meramec Caverns .... pg. 107
North County Recreation Complex .... pg. 36
Serendipity Ice Cream .... pg. 43
Wapelhorst Aquatic Facility .... pg. 38

TOP 5 DAD/CHILD FULL-DAY ACTIVITIES

Big Shark Bicycle Company .... pg. 44
Cahokia Mounds .... pg. 105
Daniel Boone Home and Boonesfield Village .... pg. 37
St. Louis Zoo .... pg. 31
Youth Activity Park .... pg. 86

TOP 5 DAD/CHILD SPLURGES $$$

Amtrak River Runner .... pg. 104
The Edge .... pg. 105
Fabulous Fox Theatre .... pg. 32
NASCAR Speedpark .... pg. 36
Swing Around Fun Town .... pg. 43

TOP 5 DAD/CHILD MOST MEMORABLE

Bender Statue Road Trip .... pg. 104
The Cave Restaurant and Resort .... pg. 105
Gateway Arch Riverboats .... pg. 29
St. Louis Carriage Company .... pg. 29
St. Louis Rams Training Camp .... pg. 108

11

THE BEST DAD/CHILD
RESTAURANTS

BAMBOO BISTRO
Downtown

214 N. 4th St.
St. Louis, MO 63102
314.241.8884 | www.bamboobistrostl.com
This Asian fusion restaurant offers a lunch buffet and friendly service; try the coconut cake for dessert as an alternative to the usual almond cookie.

BROADWAY OYSTER BAR
Downtown

736 S. Broadway Ave.
St. Louis, MO 63102
314.621.8811 | www.broadwayoysterbar.com
A unique cajun-creole hotspot in downtown St. Louis, there's no other place like it. The funky atmosphere and food choices are guaranteed to create a memorable impression. Try the shrimp grinder or po'boy and cajun chips.

CROWN CANDY KITCHEN
Downtown

1401 St. Louis Ave.
St. Louis, MO 63106
314.621.9650 | www.crowncandykitchen.net
One of St. Louis's oldest and most popular eateries, you'll feel like you've stepped back in time. The staff is friendly and more than happy to offer suggestions. Crown Candy is open for lunch and dinner and famous for its malts, shakes and candy.

THE LONDON TEA ROOM
Downtown

1520 Washington Ave.
St. Louis, MO 63103
314.241.6556 | www.thelondontearoom.com
Make your daughter feel like a princess by dressing up a bit and bonding over a spot of tea at this downtown café. As expected, the menu boasts a wide array of assorted teas along with pastries and light fare; reservations required for afternoon tea.

OLD SPAGHETTI FACTORY
Downtown

727 N. 1st St.
St. Louis, MO 63102
314.621.0276 | www.osf.com

Named one of the 10 Best Family Restaurants by Parents magazine, no tour of downtown St. Louis is complete without a stop at the Old Spaghetti Factory. Enjoy classic spaghetti and meat sauce or try something a little different like spaghetti with Mizithra cheese and browned butter. Be on the lookout for a balloon artist roaming around creating spectacular balloon animals.

The Best Dad/Child Restaurants

EINSTEIN BROS.
Forest Park & Central West End
2 N. Euclid Ave.
St. Louis, MO 63108
314.367.7999 | www.einsteinbros.com
This casual and friendly café offers 20 types of bagels and an impressive array of signature schmears and sandwiches, making it a perfect stop for breakfast or a light lunch.

FOREST PARK BOATHOUSE
Forest Park & Central West End
6101 Government Dr.
St Louis, MO 63110
314.367.2224 | www.boathouseforestpark.com
The Boathouse is pet-friendly and a perfect place to eat while spending the day in Forest Park. The atmosphere is one-of-a-kind with a massive fireplace for the winter months and a lovely view of the pond (and ducks) from the outdoor patio when the weather turns warm. The place fills up fast so it's best to call ahead for reservations on the weekends.

THE PAINTED GIRAFFE
Forest Park & Central West End
1 Government Dr.
St. Louis, Missouri 63110
314.781.0900 | www.stlzoo.org
Located in the world-famous St. Louis Zoo and featuring an extensive menu, kids' meals come with a 16oz. souvenir cup.

PICKLES DELI
Forest Park & Central West End
22 N. Euclid Ave.
St. Louis, MO 63108
314.361.DELI | www.picklesdelistl.com
Pickles Deli has been voted #1 delicatessen in St. Louis for good reason. Create your own sandwich masterpiece or try one of the specialties like the Cuban or Classic Meatball. Pickles is closed on Sundays.

RACANELLI'S NEW YORK PIZZERIA
Forest Park & Central West End
12 S. Euclid Ave.
St. Louis, MO 63108
314.367.7866 | www.racanellis.com
Racanelli's offers New York style pizza, hand tossed and baked in a brick oven, available as whole pies or by the slice. Everything is made from scratch fresh daily and there's no shortage of meaty toppings. Try the tasty garlic knots as an appetizer.

CAFÉ VENTANA
Grand Center & Midtown
3919 W. Pine Blvd.
St. Louis, MO 63108
314.531.7500 | www.cafeventana.com
You'll feel like you've walked into a bistro in New Orleans' famous French Quarter. Café Ventana is the perfect place for beignets at breakfast. For a real treat, come for brunch on the weekend and enjoy the accompaniment of live jazz musicians.

CHUY ARZOLA'S
Grand Center & Midtown
3701 Lindell Blvd. at The Coronado
St. Louis, MO 63108
314.644.4430 | www.chuyarzolas.com
Chuy Arzola's has won many awards for its spectacular Tex-Mex menu, which includes always popular sizzling fajitas and delicious tacos. Happy hour specials include $3.00 appetizers from 3 to 7pm, Monday through Friday.

CITY DINER AT THE FOX
Grand Center & Midtown
541 N. Grand Blvd.
St. Louis, MO 63103
314.533.7500 | www.saucemagazine.com/citydiner
The City Diner's second location is perfect for grabbing a burger (or even breakfast) before or after a show at the Fox Theater. This location boasts the same charm and atmosphere as the original location.

NADOZ EURO BAKERY & CAFÉ
Grand Center & Midtown
3701 Lindell Blvd. at The Coronado
St. Louis, MO 63108
314.446.6800 | www.nadozcafe.com
Make a reservation for the spectacular Sunday brunch or pop in for a delicious homemade dessert. As an added bonus, you can order a loaf of bread or pretzel rolls to take home.

PAPPY'S SMOKE HOUSE
Grand Center & Midtown
3106 Olive St.
St. Louis, MO 63103
314.535.4340 | www.pappyssmokehouse.com
Just South of Grand Center, come experience some of the best barbeque St. Louis has to offer. Pappy's is known for its generous portions and fast and friendly service. Come early; Pappy's sells out fast.

The Best Dad/Child Restaurants

ALMONDS RESTAURANT
Mid County
8127 Maryland Ave.
Clayton, MO 63105
314.725.1019 | www.almondsrestaurant.com
Open for lunch and dinner, Almonds is a family restaurant offering delicious, affordable southern comfort food in a homey atmosphere. Kids will love the pizza and quesadillas cooked in their wood-fired oven. Owners Tony and Kelli are at the restaurant welcoming diners on most evenings. It's recommended to call ahead for reservations.

CICI'S PIZZA
Mid County
9745 Manchester Rd.
Rock Hill, MO 63119
314.963.7200 | www.cicispizza.com
Cici's offers an affordable, quality pizza buffet that kids and adults will both find delicious. A great value for all, and kids under 3 eat free every day.

DICKEY'S BARBECUE PIT
Mid County
1912 S. Brentwood Blvd.
Brentwood, MO 63144
314.961.6699 | www.dickeys.com
Dickey's offers up plentiful portions of delicious barbecue and other kid favorites; kids 12 and under eat free on Sundays, and kids' meals always come with free ice cream.

O'CHARLEY'S
Mid County
1242 S. Kirkwood Rd.
Kirkwood, MO 63122
314.822.1066 | www.ocharleys.com
Enjoy delicious hot, fresh rolls on the house while dinner is cooking. O'Charley's is a great place for families to come together and enjoy each other's company; kids eat free with adult entrée purchase, so you can enjoy the delicious prime rib philly while the kids chow down on chicken strips.

POSH NOSH DELI
Mid County
8115 Maryland Ave.
St. Louis, MO 63105-3720
314.862.1890 | www.poshnoshdeli.com
Posh Nosh is an authentic deli that's open for breakfast and lunch. Try the hot corned beef on a kaiser roll, and don't forget the yummy buckets of pickles. Both indoor and outdoor seating is available, weather permitting.

DAVE AND BUSTER'S

North County

13857 Riverport Dr.
St. Louis, MO 63043
314.209.8015 | www.daveandbusters.com

Food and fun come together at Dave and Buster's. Featuring arcade, racing, and skill games galore, kids and adults can play for fun and prizes while enjoying traditional American cuisine. Specials include discounted game cards with certain meals.

INTERNATIONAL HOUSE OF PANCAKES (IHOP)

North County

11237 St. Charles Rock Rd.
Bridgeton, MO 63044-2702
314.739.6964 | www.ihop.com

Something as simple as having breakfast for dinner can often form the basis of cherished memories, and IHOP is perfect when you're in the mood for pancakes, regardless of what time it is. Kids eat free with adult purchase.

JOHNNY ROCKETS

North County

5555 St. Louis Mills Blvd.
Hazelwood, MO 63042
314.227.5303 | www.johnnyrockets.com

Johnny Rockets offers a fun diner atmosphere and the ever-popular combination of juicy burgers, fries and shakes. Tabletop jukeboxes play your favorite tunes for a nickel.

MALONE'S NEIGHBORHOOD BAR AND GRILL

North County

3336 Pershall Rd.
Ferguson, MO 63135
314.522.4300 | www.malonesgrillandpub.com

With a menu consisting of top-notch American fare including sandwiches, fire-grilled burgers, steaks and ribs, it's a toss-up regarding what's better: the food or the fact that kids eat free with adult purchase.

STEAK 'N SHAKE

North County

6050 Howdershell Rd.
Hazelwood, MO 63042
314.266.1184 | www.steaknshake.com

Kids will love the diner ambience and classic eats that include famous steakburgers with pickles sliced the long way, milkshakes and shoestring potato french fries. Kids eat free on Saturdays and Sundays; one free kids' plate for every $8 spent.

The Best Dad/Child Restaurants

ALLIN'S DINER
St. Charles

130 N. Kingshighway St.
St. Charles, MO 63301
636.946.5556

Setting this family-owned diner apart from all others is not only the quality and friendly atmosphere, but also the lack of a fryer, meaning that french fries are out; kids might protest at first, but the healthier alternatives are so good that they'll be begging to come back soon. Allin's is open for lunch throughout the week and dinner on the weekends.

INCREDIBLE PIZZA COMPANY
St. Charles

4105 N. Cloverleaf Dr.
St. Peters, MO 63376
636.477.2700 | www.ipcstlouis.com

What's a better combination than pizza and games? How about a bountiful pizza buffet that's impressive enough in its own right, but even more so when partnered with glow in the dark mini-golf, bumper cars, go-kart races, a game room and Tiny Town for younger kids.

LOCOS GRILL AND PUB
St. Charles

3803 Elm St.
St. Charles, MO 63301
636.916.4888 | www.locosgrill.com

Gigantic burritos, specialty sandwiches and amazing hot wings are among the menu choices for adults, while kids can enjoy mini corndogs, cheeseburgers, chicken tenders or other popular items from the Little League menu. Kids eat free with paying adult, Mondays through Thursdays.

MONKEY JOE'S
St. Charles

280 Megan Ave.
O'Fallon, MO 63366
636.978.5637 | www.monkeyjoes.com

This inflatable play area will really bring out the monkey in your kids without driving you bananas. Menu includes pizza and snacks, but your kids may not want to stop playing long enough to eat. Establishment is safe and clean with supervision and separate bouncing areas for different age groups. Open for walk-ins, or schedule an unforgettable birthday party.

PIZZA STREET
St. Charles

6111 Mid Rivers Mall Dr.
St. Charles, MO 63304
636.922.5588 | www.pizzastreetinc.com

Pizza Street combines great value with tons of fun, offering a $2.99 pizza buffet for kids under 10; kids under 3 eat free every day. Best of all, kids can take a break from the buffet in the game room. Ice cream cone and balloon are included with kid's buffet.

HODAK'S RESTAURANT AND BAR
Soulard & Cherokee Street
2100 Gravois Ave.
St. Louis, MO 63104
314.776.7292 | www.hodaks.com

When you talk fried chicken in St. Louis, the conversation usually begins and ends with Hodak's. The portion sizes and quality are the stuff of legend, and bulk rates are available when you want to carry-out and feed a crowd.

LA VALLESENA
Soulard & Cherokee Street
2801 Cherokee St.
St. Louis, MO 63118-3015
314.776.4223

This charming and colorful roadside café offers the best authentic tacos in St. Louis and a great value for the price. Go when the weather's warm and take advantage of the patio seating, and be sure to stop at La Vallesena 2, their storefront across the street that serves up homemade ice cream and Mexican popsicles.

THE LEMP MANSION RESTAURANT AND INN
Soulard & Cherokee Street
3322 DeMenil Pl.
St. Louis, MO 63118
314.664.8024 | www.lempmansion.com/restaurant.html

Follow up a tour of nearby Cherokee Street with an elegant and unforgettable lunch or dinner at the charming and historic (and possibly haunted) Lemp Mansion. Sundays offer the best value with "all you care to eat" Family Style dining.

LUVY DUVY'S CAFÉ
Soulard & Cherokee Street
2321 Arsenal St.
St. Louis, MO 63118
314.776.5889 | www.luvyduvys.com

Kids, pets and even grownups are all welcome to take part in the fun and happy atmosphere that Luvy Duvy's name implies; enjoy your favorite comfort food on their welcoming outdoor patio and take advantage of their renowned breakfasts being served all day on Saturdays.

The Best Dad/Child Restaurants

O'MALLEY'S
Soulard & Cherokee Street
1900 Cherokee St.
St. Louis, MO 63118
314.762.9308

O'Malley's is fondly known for its cozy Irish atmosphere and amazing corned beef and potato soup. Stop by and let Tommy and Janice treat you like you're part of the family. Keep an eye out for their bulldog mascot, Tank, as he's known to make the rounds looking for someone to pet him.

CITY DINER
South City
3139 S. Grand Blvd.
St. Louis, MO 63118
314.772.6100 | www.saucemagazine.com/citydiner

Chock full of old-fashioned diner appeal, City Diner serves up comfort food made from scratch and breakfast all day. Fun and friendly, it's easy to see why City Diner is consistently voted one of the best diners in St. Louis.

EL PAISANO
South City
3315 Watson Rd.
St. Louis, MO 63139
314.645.7455

Featuring delicious authentic Mexican food, El Paisano is very kid-friendly with crayons and coloring books provided, free chips and salsa and, best of all, a roving mariachi band.

GRBIC
South City
4071 Keokuk St.
St. Louis, MO 63116
314.772.3100 | www.grbicrestaurant.com

For something different from the standard burgers and fries, try this Bosnian/Eastern European restaurant that's very accommodating of newborns and young kids; in addition to the authentic and eclectic ethnic offerings, more traditional fare is also available.

IRON BARLEY
South City
5510 Virginia Ave.
St. Louis, MO 63111
314.351.4500 | www.ironbarley.com

Kitschy and eclectic, Iron Barley has been featured on the Food Network's Diners, Drive-ins and Dives, and the Travel Channel's Man vs. Food. The food is traditional with a twist, and everyone's welcome to enjoy the atmosphere and menu options.

TIN CAN TAVERN
South City

3157 Morganford Rd.
St. Louis, MO 63116
314.865.3003 | www.tincantavern.com

Featuring a simple yet diverse menu consisting of comfort food and American homestyle specialties, the food at the Tin Can Tavern earns the many accolades it receives. Kids 10 and under eat free from 5 to 9pm, Monday through Thursday.

FORTEL'S PIZZA DEN
South County

7932 Mackenzie Rd.
St. Louis, MO 63123
314.353.2360 | www.fortelspizzaden.com

One of the area's best "mom and pop" pizza joints, everything is guaranteed to be fresh and delicious, including the made from scratch pizza dough. Kids can enjoy playing arcade games while they wait, and the outdoor patio is perfect on a warm night.

FUDDRUCKERS
South County

10752 Sunset Hills Plaza
St Louis, MO 63127-1289
314.966.3833 | www.fuddruckers.com

Fuddruckers bills itself as the home of the world's greatest hamburgers, and few would argue. Kids will enjoy adding their favorite toppings at the fresh fixins bar, and the thick cut seasoned fries go perfect with cheese sauce. For the more adventurous diner, the expanded menu also includes exotic burgers such as buffalo, elk and wild boar. Kids eat for .99 on Tuesday and Wednesday after 4pm, and no trip to Fuddruckers is complete without a fresh chocolate-chip cookie to finish things off.

HAPPY JOE'S
South County

7918 Watson Rd.
St. Louis, MO 63119
314.961.4074 | www.happyjoes.com

Happy Joe's is a St. Louis institution and the perfect place to gather the family together for pizza and fun. The Mexican pizza is their specialty, and don't forget to save room for ice cream. Kids can enjoy the game area and compete for prizes. Go on your birthday to be serenaded in style by the enthusiastic, if not necessarily on key, staff.

THE PASTA HOUSE COMPANY
South County

6214 S. Lindbergh Blvd.
St. Louis, MO 63123
314.894.9161 | www.pastahouse.com

A respected Italian restaurant that treats kids with the respect and consideration they deserve, the children's menu features selections and portion sizes that are just right. Kids 12 and under eat free on Sundays with paying adults.

The Best Dad/Child Restaurants

SMUGALAS PIZZA
South County
10150 Watson Rd.
St. Louis, MO 63127
314.842.5900 | www.smugalas.com

Tasty thin crust pizza, famous chicken wings and a game room consisting of arcade and skill games make this South County spot a family favorite. Specials are offered throughout the week and whenever St. Louis sports teams play. Patio dining is a perfect option when the weather is nice or when the volume starts to reach uncomfortable levels inside.

BLUEBERRY HILL
University City
6504 Delmar Blvd.
St. Louis, MO 63130
314.727.4444 | www.blueberryhill.com

Located in the one-of-a-kind Delmar Loop, Blueberry Hill is the perfect place to find your thrill and famous for its great hamburgers, extensive jukebox, and kitschy atmosphere that includes lots of funky toys and collectibles throughout the restaurant. The walls are adorned with pictures of owner Joe Edwards with his many famous friends; how many do your kids recognize?

FITZ'S ROOTBEER
University City
6605 Delmar Blvd.
St. Louis, MO 63130-4504
314.726.9555 | www.fitzsrootbeer.com

Fitz's loves kids and vice versa. Unlike any restaurant you've ever been to, Fitz's features not only a fun atmosphere and great food, but also an authentic root beer bottling line. Kid's meals are served in mini-autos, and don't forget the root beer floats, of course. As an added bonus, kids who finish their float get a cool refrigerator magnet to take home.

FRANK AND HELEN'S PIZZERIA
University City
8111 Olive Blvd.
University City, MO 63130
314.997.0666 | www.frankandhelens.com

Frank and Helen's is a genuine family restaurant in every sense of the word. Offerings include pizza, Italian specialties and genuine broasted chicken. Kids eat free with adult entrée purchase, Tuesday through Thursday after 5pm.

23

LU LU
University City

8224 Olive Blvd.
University City, MO 63130
314.997.3108 | www.luluseafood.com

This popular Chinese restaurant focuses on the importance of both family and food: The food is guaranteed to be authentic and you'll always be treated as part of the family. Kids will enjoy broadening their tastebuds' horizons as they share small to medium portions of dim sum.

PAM'S CHICAGO DOGS AND MORE
University City

6016 Delmar Blvd.
St Louis, MO 63130
314.721.PAMS | www.pamscsd.com

Pam's is home to the best hot dogs in St. Louis, offering everything from gourmet hotdogs to veggie dogs and gyros. If you're feeling particularly adventurous, you can try the deep fried Twinkie for dessert.

HUHOT MONGOLIAN GRILL
West County

12675 Olive Blvd.
St. Louis, MO 63141
314.392.9696 | www.huhot.com/Locations/Missouri/Creve_Coeur

Who doesn't love Mongolian barbecue? Kids control their dinner destiny as they fill their bowl with fresh meats, noodles and veggies, and then watch as it's all cooked on a gigantic steaming grill right before their eyes. Kids 10 and under eat free on Tuesday nights.

JOE BOCCARDI'S
West County

128 Boccardi Ln.
Eureka, MO 63025
636.938.6100 | www.boccardis.com

It's not uncommon to see owner Joe Boccardi hanging around at dinnertime, making sure that everything's running smoothly and that everyone's well taken care of. The St. Louis style pizza comes on a thin crust with fresh, delicious toppings, and kids will like eating on the outdoor patio on a nice night.

KRIEGER'S SPORTS GRILL
West County

1684 Clarkson Rd.
Chesterfield, MO 63017
636.530.1996 | www.kriegerssportsgrill.com

A fun atmosphere and great food, Krieger's features a revamped and extensive menu. Lots of TVs to watch your favorite game, and kids 10 and under eat free on Tuesdays with adult purchase.

The Best Dad/Child Restaurants

NICOLETTI'S STEAK AND PASTA   West County

1366 Big Bend Sq. Shop Ctr.
Ballwin, MO 63021
636.225.4222

It's not uncommon for the owner to stop by your table and make sure you're enjoying your meal at this family-owned Italian restaurant. Favorites include pasta and pizza, and kids 10 and under eat free with every adult meal purchased on Tuesdays and Wednesdays.

PHIL'S BBQ   West County

115 W. 5th St.
Eureka, MO 63025-1109
636.938.6575

One of Eureka's oldest family-owned restaurants, Phil's may not be fancy, but it sure is friendly and welcoming. Large portions of barbecue are served slathered in sauce, and Phil will go out of his way to entertain the entire family and ensure that everyone has a good time and leaves full.

THE BEST DAD/CHILD
ACTIVITIES

CITY MUSEUM
Downtown

701 N. 15th St.
St. Louis, MO 63103
314.231.CITY | www.CityMuseum.org

A testament to the power of imagination, City Museum is a can't-miss destination. From the bizarre and inventive MonstroCity climbing area and World's Largest Pencil to the twisting and turning of the Enchanted Caves and the World Aquarium (snakes and stingrays and otters, oh my), City Museum has something for kids (and adults) of all ages. And yes, that is an old school bus on the roof.

EUGENE FIELD HOUSE AND THE ST. LOUIS TOY MUSEUM
Downtown

634 S. Broadway
St. Louis, MO 63102
314.421.4689 | www.eugenefieldhouse.org

A national historic landmark, the Eugene Field House was home to noted children's poet and essayist Eugene Field. Come during the holiday season to see the house decorated in 19th century finery. Open 7 days a week, but appointments are required on Monday and Tuesday (and every day in January and February).

FLAMINGO BOWL
Downtown

1117 Washington Ave.
St. Louis, MO 63101
314.436.6666 | www.flamingobowl.net

A quirky 12-lane bowling alley that's fun for kids and adults, Flamingo Bowl boasts an eclectic menu that blows away the old "hot dogs and fries" fare typical of bowling alleys and an extensive drink menu for grownups. Kids 16 and under welcome prior to 9 pm, but must be accompanied by an adult. Reduced rates are offered on shoe rentals for kids 12 and under.

GATEWAY ARCH AND MUSEUM OF WESTWARD EXPANSION
Downtown

119 N. Leonor K Sullivan Blvd.
St. Louis, MO 63102
314.982.1410 | www.gatewayarch.com/Arch

Climb inside the Arch and take a tram to the top to enjoy the breathtaking view of the city and the Mississippi river stretching out below you. After riding to the top, head in the opposite direction and go underneath to the Museum of Westward Expansion for a glimpse into the past and the world that Lewis and Clark explored on their famous trek west. General admission is free but tickets are required to ride to the top of the Arch.

GATEWAY ARCH RIVERBOATS   Downtown
50 Leonor K. Sullivan Blvd.
St. Louis, MO 63102
877.982.1410
www.coreofdiscovery.com/explore/gateway-arch-riverboat-cruises
Cruise down the Mississippi and sightsee in style from the deck of a replica 19th century paddle-wheel boat. One-hour, dinner and specialty cruises available.

THE GRIOT MUSEUM OF BLACK HISTORY AND CULTURE   Downtown
2505 St. Louis Ave.
St. Louis, MO 63106
314.241.7057 | www.thegriotmuseum.com
The Griot's vision is to be "the premier resource for Black history and culture in the Midwest." It contains life-size wax figures, an authentic slave cabin, art, artifacts and more. Museum is closed on Sundays.

ST. LOUIS CARRIAGE COMPANY   Downtown
1000 Cerre St.
St. Louis, MO 63102
314.621.3334 | www.stlouiscarriagecompany.com
Why walk when you can ride around in style? Regal Percheron draft horses provide the horsepower for these beautiful carriages. Horse-drawn carriage rides are available nightly.

SCOTT JOPLIN HOUSE   Downtown
2658 Delmar Blvd.
St. Louis, MO 63103
314.340.5790 | www.mostateparks.com/scottjoplin.htm
Tour the house of Scott Joplin, the "King of Ragtime," where some of the most famous ragtime classics of all time were composed. Children 5 and under free.

SOLDIERS MEMORIAL MILITARY MUSEUM   Downtown
1315 Chestnut St.
St. Louis, MO 63103
314.622.4550 | www.stlsoldiersmemorial.org
The site that would eventually house the Soldiers Memorial building was dedicated by President Franklin D. Roosevelt in 1926. Objects on display in the museum relate to the wartime and military experience, both local and national, and are rotated regularly. Admission is free.

UPPER LIMITS
Downtown

326 S. 21st St.
St. Louis, MO 63103
314.241.ROCK | www.upperlimits.com

Experience the thrill of rock climbing in a fun and safe environment. Courses are designed for beginning, intermediate and experienced climbers. An exciting full body workout, exercise never seemed so fun.

BOATHOUSE IN FOREST PARK
Forest Park & Central West End

6101 Government Dr.
St. Louis, MO 63110
314.367.2224 | www.boathouseforestpark.com

Rent a paddleboat or kayak and spend a spring afternoon on Post-Dispatch lake in Forest Park. Don't worry – the ducks, geese, fish and turtles welcome the company.

CATHEDRAL BASILICA OF ST. LOUIS
Forest Park & Central West End

Lindell Blvd. at Newstead Ave.
St. Louis, MO 63108
314.373.8240 | www.cathedralstl.org

A breathtaking masterpiece of art and history, come see beautiful mosaics depicting the interaction of God and humanity. Guided tours are available by appointment, Monday through Friday, and the amazingly talented Cathedral Choir sings at the 10am Sunday Mass.

MISSOURI HISTORY MUSEUM
Forest Park & Central West End

5700 Lindell Blvd.
St. Louis, MO 63112
314.746.4599 | www.mohistory.org

Learning about Missouri's history can be fun for kids and adults both. Everything from the 1904 World's Fair to Miles Davis and the Cardinals, general admission is free. Also, the Museum offers more than 500 special events throughout the year; check out their website for more details.

THE MUNY
Forest Park & Central West End

1 Theater Dr.
St. Louis, MO 63112
314.361.1900 | www.muny.org

Enjoy musical theatre under the stars. A favorite summertime tradition, get there early to claim some of the free seats. The 2011 season includes The Little Mermaid, Bye Bye Birdie and other family favorites.

The Best Dad/Child Activities

ST. LOUIS ART MUSEUM
Forest Park & Central West End

1 Fine Arts Dr.
St. Louis, MO 63110-1380
314.721.0072 | www.slam.org

Carved above the main entryway is the inscription "Dedicated to Art and Free to All." Nearly every culture and historical period is represented in the Museum's many collections. It's easy to get lost inside, in a good way. Museum is closed on Mondays.

ST. LOUIS SCIENCE CENTER & OMNIMAX THEATER
Forest Park & Central West End

5050 Oakland Ave.
St. Louis, MO 63110
314.289.4400 | www.slsc.org

General admission to the Science Center is free, but tickets are required for some special attractions and shows at the OMNIMAX Theater. Kids will love standing on the enclosed overpass and using radar guns on traffic whizzing by on Hwy. 40. And don't worry about the giant T-Rex; his growl is worse than his bite.

ST. LOUIS ZOO
Forest Park & Central West End

1 Government Dr.
St. Louis, MO 63110
314.781.0900 | www.stlzoo.org

Arguably the best free zoo in the United States and home to many large, interactive exhibits and 700 species of animals. Some of the attractions require a fee, but many are free during the first hour the Zoo is open.

STEINBERG SKATING RINK
Forest Park & Central West End

400 Jefferson Dr.
St. Louis, MO 63110
314.367.7465 | www.steinbergskatingrink.com

Located in Forest Park and open every day, even holidays, from mid-November through early March. Skate admission is valid all day, so you can take a break and enjoy the rest of Forest Park's attractions between laps around the rink.

THIRD DEGREE GLASS FACTORY
Forest Park & Central West End
5200 Delmar Blvd.
St. Louis, MO 63108
314.367.4527 | www.thirddegreeglassfactory.com

Awesome glass art is on display. Stop by Monday through Saturday to watch artists work or check out the free monthly open house the third Friday of every month from 6 to 10pm for demonstrations, activities and music.

CIRCUS FLORA
Grand Center & Midtown
634 N. Grand Blvd. #10A
St. Louis, MO 63103-1025
314.533.1285 | www.circusflora.org

Circus Flora is like no other circus and world famous for a reason. Once a year Circus Flora sets up its big top tent in the parking lot of Powell Hall and astounds audiences with its unique one-ring show, a thematic event featuring renowned local and traveling performers and animals.

CONTEMPORARY ART MUSEUM
Grand Center & Midtown
3750 Washington Blvd.
St. Louis, MO 63108
314.535.4660 | www.camstl.org

The Contemporary Art Museum features art exhibits that change three to four times a year. Children's admission is free. The Museum is closed on Monday and Tuesday.

DANCE ST. LOUIS
Grand Center & Midtown
3547 Olive St.
St. Louis, MO 63103
314.534.6622 | www.dancestlouis.org

Dance St. Louis has been thrilling St. Louis audiences for 44 years. The always popular STOMP will be returning in March 2011 and tickets are sure to go fast. Discounted tickets are available for most programs for kids under 12.

FABULOUS FOX THEATRE
Grand Center & Midtown
527 N. Grand Blvd.
St. Louis, MO 63103
314.535.1700 | www.fabulousfox.com

The beautiful and awe-inspiring Fox Theatre is a wonder to behold, even when the stage is empty. The ornate surroundings contribute to an amazing experience and unforgettable trip to the theatre. Disney's Imagination Movers will be appearing in March 2011.

The Best Dad/Child Activities

THE FOUNTAIN ON LOCUST
Grand Center & Midtown
3037 Locust Blvd.
St. Louis, MO 63103
314.535.7800 | www.fountainonlocust.com
Kids will love the ice cream selections and the handpainted art-deco interior, while you'll love the fact that The Fountain on Locust boasts the best bathrooms in St. Louis, making it a safe bet for when the little ones start frantically tugging on your pant leg.

GRANDEL THEATRE
Grand Center & Midtown
3610 Grandel Sq.
St. Louis, MO 63108
314.534.1834 | www.grandcenter.org/grandel
Both the St. Louis Black Repertory Company and the St. Louis Shakespeare Company perform at the Grandel Theatre, which is known for its intimate and laid-back atmosphere; the theatre also hosts other local and national acts.

MOOLAH THEATER AND LOUNGE
Grand Center & Midtown
3821 Lindell Blvd.
St. Louis, MO 63108
314.446.6806 | www.stlouiscinemas.com/moolah
When you want to go the movies in style, skip the cineplex and head to the Moolah. Get there early to snag a spot on one of the comfy couches. After the movie, head downstairs to the retro bowling alley.

MOTO MUSEUM
Grand Center & Midtown
3441 Olive St.
St. Louis, MO 63103-1144
314.446.1805 | www.themotomuseum.com
The Moto Museum consists of an impressive collection of rare and vintage motorcycles. General admission is free. The museum is closed Saturday and Sunday.

PORTFOLIO GALLERY AND EDUCATION CENTER
Grand Center & Midtown
3514 Delmar Blvd.
St. Louis, MO 63103
314.533.3323 | www.portfoliogallerystl.org
Portfolio Gallery is a welcoming, friendly art gallery that features exhibits by local and national African-American artists. Free and open to the public on Monday, Wednesday and Friday (Tuesday and Thursday by appointment only).

ST. LOUIS SYMPHONY ORCHESTRA — Grand Center & Midtown

718 N. Grand Blvd.
St. Louis, MO 63103
314.534.1700 | www.stlsymphony.org

The St. Louis Symphony Orchestra offers family concerts on four Sundays throughout the season, including the timeless classic Peter and the Wolf. Check their website for scheduling. Recommended for kids ages 5 and up.

HOME DEPOT KIDS WORKSHOP — Mid County

1603 S. Hanley Rd.
Brentwood, MO 63144
314.647.6050 | www.homedepot.com — Seach "Kids Workshop"

Home Depot offers free, hands-on workshops on the first Saturday of every month. Designed for kids ages 5 and up, dads and kids can build together and keep the completed project kit.

LITTLE FISHES SWIM SCHOOL — Mid County

8200 Brentwood Industrial Dr.
Brentwood, MO 63144
314.647.SWIM | www.littlefishesswimschool.com

The benefit of a heated, indoor pool is that swimming lessons can be offered year-round. Professional staff offers fun and safe age-appropriate lessons. The pool is also available for parties.

MAD SCIENCE — Mid County

8420 Olive Blvd., Suite R
St. Louis, MO 63132
314.991.8000 | www.madscience.org

Mad Science of St. Louis offers Summer Camps, after-school workshops and amazing birthday parties. Shows are interactive, high-energy and almost too much fun to be considered educational.

MAGIC HOUSE — Mid County

516 S. Kirkwood Rd.
St. Louis, MO 63122
314.822.8900 | www.magichouse.org

Hundreds of interactive exhibits beckon throughout the Magic House Children's Museum, guaranteeing your children will be happy and exhausted by the time the day is done. Kids love the static electricity ball and surrounding themselves with a giant bubble in the bubble room.

The Best Dad/Child Activities

ST. LOUIS COUNTY LIBRARY MID COUNTY BRANCH
Mid County

7821 Maryland Ave.
St. Louis, MO 63105
314.721.3008 | www.slcl.org/branches/mc
Story time is held every Wednesday at 10am for kids 2-5 years. The library also hosts lots of other cool events throughout the year. Free.

SHARK FITNESS TRAINING
Mid County

314.822.2773 | www.sharkfitness.net
Shark Fitness Training offers family boot camps on Saturdays at various locations throughout St. Louis. This is a serious workout and only for those who are willing to work hard.

STAGES ST. LOUIS
Mid County

111 S. Geyer Rd.
Kirkwood, MO 63122
314.821.2407 | www.stagesstlouis.com
Sign your son or daughter up for dance and theater classes or take in a show together. Stages will be performing The Secret Garden and Disney's 101 Dalmations as part of the 2011 series.

CHALLENGER LEARNING CENTER IN ST. LOUIS
North County

205 Brotherton Ln.
St. Louis, MO 63135
314.521.6205 | www.clcstlouis.org
2011 marks the 25th anniversary of the space shuttle Challenger disaster, and the Challenger Learning Center is commemorating the occasion with a host of programs and activities designed to educate the public and honor the memory of the astronauts who lost their lives in the explosion. Reservations are recommended for simulated space missions.

FAMILY JUMP CENTER
North County

5555 St Louis Mills Blvd. #634
Hazelwood, MO 63042-4433
314.227.5157 | www.familyjumpcenter.com
This inflatable play center in the St. Louis Mills Mall is great for birthday parties or for when your kids just need to jump, bounce and slide.

FIRST DUE FIRE MUSEUM
North County

5555 St. Louis Mills Blvd.
Hazelwood, MO 63042-4433
314.227.5911 | www.firstduefiremuseum.com

This one-of-a-kind museum in the St. Louis Mills Mall promotes fire safety in a fun, interactive way while displaying fire service memorabilia. Admission is free, but $1 lets your kids ring the fire bell. Open Friday through Sunday.

NASCAR SPEEDPARK
North County

5555 St Louis Mills Blvd. #375
Hazelwood, MO 63042-4433
314.227.5600 | www.nascarspeedpark.com

What kid doesn't want to get behind the wheel and take a spin? While there are lots of fun activities to choose from at NASCAR Speedpark, including rock climbing, laser tag and bumper boats, the highlight is the race cars and multiple tracks.

NORTH COUNTY RECREATION COMPLEX
North County

2577 Redman Rd.
St. Louis, MO 63136
314.615.8840
www.stlouisco.com/parks/NorthCountyRecreationComplex.html

The North County Recreation Complex includes a golf course, outdoor pool, gymnasium, playground, tennis courts and fishing pond. Admission is free for kids 4 and under.

PUTTING EDGE
North County

5555 St Louis Mills Blvd. #459
Hazelwood, MO 63042-4433
314.291.7600 | www.puttingedge.com

The Putting Edge features glow in the dark mini golf and arcades. Kids will love the neon surroundings and upbeat music that characterize this alternative to standard mini golf. This is a great option when considering birthday party ideas.

ST. LOUIS BALLET
North County

Blanche M. Touhill Performing Arts Center
1 University Blvd.
St. Louis, MO 63121-4400
314.516.4949 | www.stlouisballet.org

If you're looking to create a perfect day out for the little girl who dreams of being a ballerina, look no further. The 2011 season includes Romeo and Juliet.

The Best Dad/Child Activities

ST. LOUIS COUNTY LIBRARY FLORISSANT VALLEY BRANCH
North County
195 New Florissant Rd. S.
Florissant, MO 63031
314.994.3300 | www.slcl.org/branches/fv
Story time is held for kids ages 3 to 5 years at 11:30am on Thursdays, with other special events scheduled throughout the week.

ADRENALINE ZONE
St. Charles
1875 Old Hwy. 94 S.
St. Charles, MO 63303
636.940.7700 | www.db-az.com/index.html
Adrenaline Zone features laser tag with a twist. Up to 3 teams of 10 players each work together in this fast-paced and exhilarating game.

BRUNSWICK ZONE XL
St. Charles
8070 Veterans Memorial Pkwy.
St. Peters, MO 63376
636.474.BOWL | www.bowlbrunswick.com
Bowling is just the tip of the iceberg at Brunswick Zone XL. Play a game of pool or laser tag and test your skills (and win prizes) in the giant game room. Schedule a birthday party and they'll take care of everything, even providing a personal "party host."

DANIEL BOONE HOME AND BOONESFIELD VILLAGE
St. Charles
1868 Hwy. F
Defiance, MO 63341
636.798.2005 | www.lindenwood.edu/boone
Instead of regaling your kids with "When I was younger..." stories, let them experience life as a frontiersman or woman. Guided tours of the Daniel Boone home and Boonesfield Village are offered daily. Admission is free for kids 3 and under.

DEMOLITION BALL
St. Charles
1875 Old Hwy. 94 S.
St. Charles, MO 63303
636.940.7700 | www.db-az.com/demolitionball.html
Demolition ball is an exciting game that combines football, basketball, polo and hockey with bumper cars. Minimum age and height requirements of 12 years and 54" apply.

DIERBERGS SCHOOL OF COOKING
St. Charles

2021 Zumbehl Rd.
St. Charles, MO 63303
636.669.0049 | www.dierbergs.com

Dierbergs offers fun and informal parent and child cooking classes in their fully functioning kitchen classrooms. Classes can also be customized for birthday parties and other special occasions.

FIRST MISSOURI STATE CAPITOL STATE HISTORIC SITE
St. Charles

200-216 S. Main St.
St. Charles, MO 63301
636.940.3322 | www.mostateparks.com/firstcapitol.htm

Prior to moving to Jefferson City, Missouri's State Capitol was seated in St. Charles. Tour the actual rooms where Missouri's state government was first formed and met. Guided tours require a fee, but admission is free for exhibits in the interpretive center.

GRAND PRIX KARTING
St. Charles

3500 MO-94
St. Charles, MO 63301
636.946.4848

If you and your kids are new to the Go-Kart scene, Grand Prix Karting is a great place to get your feet wet; the price is reasonable, staff is friendly, and it's usually not very crowded. Single or double karts are available.

SANTA PARADE
St. Charles

S. Main St.
St. Charles, MO 63301
www.stcharleschristmas.com/santaparade.htm

Christmas in St. Charles isn't complete without the Santa Parade. The Parade takes place on opening day (end of November) and every Saturday and Sunday of the annual Christmas Traditions festival. The Parade consists of Victorian carolers, legends of Christmas and multiple representations of Santa.

WAPELHORST AQUATIC FACILITY
St. Charles

1874 Muegge Rd.
St. Charles, MO 63303
636.936.8118 | www.stcharlesparks.com

When the dog days of summer roll around, your best option is Wapelhorst Aquatic Facility. Not only will you and your kids get to cool off, but you can also enjoy thrilling rides like the 5 story speed slide. For the best value, go on a Sunday when ticket prices are reduced from 5 to 7pm.

The Best Dad/Child Activities

ANHEUSER-BUSCH BREWERY TOURS
Soulard & Cherokee Street
12th & Lynch St.
St. Louis, MO 63118
314.577.2626 | www.budweisertours.com/toursSTL.htm
In addition to the Beechwood Lager Cellars and historic Brew House, tours also include a walk through the Clydesdale Stable, home of those famous horses. Come during the holidays, when over one million lights are on display. Free tour includes product sampling for those over 21 years of age.

BEGGIN' PET PARADE
Soulard & Cherokee Street
Allen Ave. & Menard St.
St. Louis, MO 63104
www.mardigrasinc.com/events/beggin-strips-barkus-pet-parade
Dress your pet in their best doggy duds and come celebrate Mardi Gras with your favorite four-legged friend. The parade's free to watch, or you can be a part of the action for a $10 registration fee.

CHEROKEE RECREATION CENTER
Soulard & Cherokee Street
3200 S. Jefferson Ave.
St. Louis, MO 63118-3102
314.664.0582
www.stlouis.missouri.org/citygov/parks/recreation_div/cherokee.html
Take advantage of the Center's workout rooms and gymnasium, and then cool down with a few laps in the indoor pool. Summer camps are also available.

GUS'S PRETZELS
Soulard & Cherokee Street
1820 Arsenal St.
St. Louis, MO 63118
314.664.4010 | www.guspretzels.com
Follow up your tour of the Anheuser-Busch brewery with a stop at Gus's for one of their world-famous, made fresh daily pretzels; kids will enjoy seeing the pretzels being made while waiting in line. Try a cinnamon-sugar stick or hotdog pretzel sandwich. Gus's is closed on Mondays.

JASPER'S ANTIQUE RADIO MUSEUM
Soulard & Cherokee Street
2022-24 Cherokee St.
St. Louis, MO 63118
314.421.8313
This eclectic and wonderfully ramshackle shop houses a huge collection of radios and related equipment, over 10,000 at last count, including antique and novelty radios.

PETSMART
WEINER DOG DERBY
Soulard & Cherokee Street

Soulard Market Park, corner of 9th St. and Lafayette Ave.
St. Louis, MO 63104
www.mardigrasinc.com/events/petsmart-wiener-dog-derby

You've never seen a race like this. Forget racecars and horses, nothing can compete with a weiner dog. This hilarious race takes place at Mardi Gras and follows the Beggin' Pet Parade. The derby is free to watch or $10 to register your dachshund as a competitor.

RAMP RIDERS
Soulard & Cherokee Street

2324 Salena St.
St. Louis, MO 63104
314.776.4025 | www.rampriders.net

This indoor skatepark, owned and operated by professionals who enjoy interacting with the skating community, is held in high esteem by local skaters and bike riders. Special beginner sessions for kids ages 2-10 are held every Sunday from 10am–noon. The fee is $10, and that includes a drink and pizza. Also, parents and siblings are invited to ride at no additional cost.

FRONTYARD FEATURES
South City

314.664.4330 | www.fyfstl.com

Front Yard Features brings movies on a big screen to parks and neighborhoods throughout St. Louis. Check the website for upcoming events or to schedule one in your neighborhood.

HOME DEPOT KIDS WORKSHOP
South City

3202 S. Kings Hwy. Blvd.
St. Louis, MO 63139
314.865.0700 | www.homedepot.com - Search Kids Workshop

Home Depot Offers free, hands-on workshops on the first Saturday of every month. Designed for kids ages 5 and up, dads and kids can build together and keep the completed project kit.

MINIATURE MUSEUM
OF GREATER ST. LOUIS
South City

4746 Gravois Ave.
St. Louis, MO 63116-2437
314.832.7790 | www.miniaturemuseum.org

On display at the Miniature Museum are an impressive collection of detailed dollhouses and other miniature replicas, including many St. Louis landmarks. Museum is closed on Mondays and Tuesdays.

The Best Dad/Child Activities

MISSOURI BOTANICAL GARDEN
South City
4344 Shaw Blvd.
St. Louis, MO 63110
314.577.5100 | www.mobot.org
This St. Louis landmark invites you to stroll through its beautiful gardens; enjoy the Climatron conservatory and Children's Garden and be sure to take time to feed the fish from the bridge over the koi pond. In addition to the regular attractions, many festivals are held throughout the year.

SAINT LOUIS CITY OPEN STUDIO AND GALLERY (SCOSAG)
South City
4255 Arsenal St.
St. Louis, MO 63116
314.865.0060 | www.scosag.org
More than just exploring the arts, Saint Louis City Open Studio and Gallery allows kids to be a part of them. SCOSaG offers classes and workshops, birthday p-ART-ies and open studio hours. The Gallery is closed on Fridays and Sundays.

SOUTH CITY FAMILY YMCA
South City
3150 Sublette Ave.
St. Louis, MO 63139
314.644.3100 | www.ymcastlouis.org
There are lots of things to do at the Y, including a wading pool, lazy river, water slides and separate area for adult swimming. Food is provided by South City restaurant Urban Eats and includes lots of healthy wraps and smoothies to choose from.

TED DREWES CONCRETE AND CHRISTMAS TREE LOT
South City
6726 Chippewa Ave.
St. Louis, MO 63109
314.481.2652 | www.teddrewes.com
Ted Drewes has long been a required stop for locals and tourists alike. Famous for its one-of-a-kind concrete frozen treats and always exceptional service, Ted Drewes is also gaining attention for its quality Christmas trees, fresh cut and hand-selected in Novia Scotia by Ted himself. Ted Drewes is the perfect starting point when creating family traditions.

BOUNCE U
South County

4403 Meramec Bottom Rd., Suite C
Saint Louis, MO 63129
314.845.7529 | www.bounceu.com

Tons of bouncing, inflatable fun in your own private environment promises a birthday your child will never forget. Parties include professional party hosts to make sure everyone has an awesome time. Open "Bounce Sessions" are also available, reservations required.

CHILDREN'S ILLUSTRATED ART MUSEUM
South County

37 Crestwood Ct.
Crestwood, MO 63126
314.941.2097 | www.stlciam.org

Kids will love seeing original art from their favorite books, including sketches, illustrations and paintings, up close. Special events and exhibitions promise a unique and amazing experience.

CONCORD ROLLERCADE SKATING RINK
South County

11703 Baptist Church Rd.
St. Louis, MO 63128
314.842.3845

A classic that never goes out of style, your kids will love a trip to the roller skating rink; be warned, however, that they might not be quite so enamored with your own reminiscences of couple skates from long ago. Concord Rollercade is available for open skating and also birthday parties.

FEED MY PEOPLE
South County

171 Kingston Dr.
St. Louis, MO 63125-2932
314.631.4900 | www.feed-my-people.org

Kids and parents can put their time and energy to good use by volunteering at this interdenominational Christian help center. Tasks might include sorting canned goods or other items that have been collected.

GRANT'S FARM
South County

10501 Gravois Rd.
St. Louis, MO 63123
314.843.1700 | www.grantsfarm.com

Hop on the tram and enjoy the narrated tour of this 281-acre ancestral home of the Busch family. Over 100 species of animals are represented, including some which you can get up close and personal with, like baby goats. Stop for lunch or a snack in the Bauernhof courtyard, where adults can enjoy complimentary Anheuser–Busch products.

The Best Dad/Child Activities

JEFFERSON BARRACKS MUSEUMS — South County
345 N. Rd.
St. Louis, MO 63125
314.544.5714 | www.co.st-louis.mo.us/parks/jb-museum.html
Tour what used to be an active U.S. Army post and learn more about the many famous Americans who served at Jefferson Barracks, including Robert E. Lee and U.S. Grant.

OPERA THEATRE OF ST. LOUIS — South County
130 Edgar Rd.
St. Louis, MO 63119
314.961.0644 | www.opera-stl.org
For something different, deck yourself out in your best suit and tie and get the kids dressed up for an evening at the opera. After the opera, you can usually mingle with the cast by the fountain on the hill.

SERENDIPITY ICE CREAM — South County
8130 Big Bend Blvd.
Webster Groves, MO 63119
314.962.2700 | www.serendipity-icecream.com
Beat the heat on a summer day by ordering a scoop or two of homemade ice cream and relaxing on the nearby grassy pavilion. Flavors change on a regular basis so you can find a new favorite each time you go.

SWING AROUND FUN TOWN — South County
141 Gravois Rd.
Fenton, MO 63026
636.349.7077 | www.swing-a-round.com
A one-stop shop for family fun that includes both indoor and outdoor activities such as bowling, a giant arcade, tunnels and slides, go karts, bumper boats, mini-golf and batting cages.

TRANSPORTATION MUSEUM — South County
3015 Barrett Station Rd.
St. Louis, MO 63122
314.965.6885 | www.museumoftransport.org
Get a move on to the Transportation Museum and explore more than 300 pieces including steam, diesel and electric locomotives, automobiles, streetcars, buses and aircraft. Kids 5 and under can enjoy the interactive Creation Station.

BIG SHARK BICYCLE COMPANY University City
6133 Delmar Blvd.
St. Louis, MO 63112
314.862.1188 | www.bigshark.com
You could take a walking tour of the Delmar Loop, or you could rent a bike from Big Shark and cruise down the street in style; rental includes free lock and helmet.

CENTER OF CREATIVE ARTS (COCA) University City
524 Trinity Ave.
St. Louis, MO 63130-4314
314.725.6555 | www.cocastl.org
COCA is arguably the number one source for creative arts education and performances in St. Louis. Sign up for a dance or music class or workshop, or enjoy a dance, comedy or musical performance as part of the audience.

CRAFT ALLIANCE University City
6640 Delmar Blvd.
St. Louis, MO 63130
314.725.1177 | www.craftalliance.org
Kids ages 3 and up can take classes in various arts and craft disciplines, including sculpting, metalworking and fiber arts. Get to class early and take some time to stroll through the gallery and check out the current exhibitions.

FRO-YO University City
6329 Delmar Blvd.
University City, MO 63130
314.862.1717 | www.froyoyogurt.com
Fro-Yo offers a funky, modern atmosphere and healthier alternative to ice cream. Create your own sundaes and pay based on the weight of your bowl.

JILLY'S CUPCAKE BAR AND CAFÉ University City
8509 Delmar Blvd.
St. Louis, MO 63124
314.993.5455 | www.jillyscupcakebar.com
Gourmet cupcakes are all the rage, and nobody does it better than Jilly's. Stop in for a treat or book a Sprinkle Party and let your daughter and her friends create their own amazing edible inventions.

The Best Dad/Child Activities

MESHUGGAH CAFÉ
University City
6269 Delmar Blvd.
St. Louis, MO 63130
314.726.5662 | www.meshuggahcafe.com
There will be no shortage of conversation when you and your son or daughter order up a cup of coffee and a smoothie, take a seat at Meshuggah's outside patio and watch the flow of people moving down the Delmar Loop; this is a great way to pass an hour or so.

ST. LOUIS PHILHARMONIC
University City
E. Desmond Lee Concert Hall
560 Trinity Ave.
University City, MO 63130
314.421.3600 | www.stlphilharmonic.org
Conveniently located near many great restaurants and attractions on the Delmar Loop, enjoy a nice dinner followed by a classical performance from the Philharmonic Orchestra.

SUBTERRANEAN BOOKS STORY TIME
University City
6275 Delmar Blvd.
St. Louis, MO
314.862.6100 | www.store.subbooks.com
Georgy Rock, known throughout St. Louis as "The Story Lady," entertains with songs and stories every Thursday from 11:30am to noon.

AMERICAN KENNEL CLUB MUSEUM OF THE DOG
West County
1721 S. Mason Rd.
Ballwin, MO 63011
314.821.3647 | www.museumofthedog.org
Located in Queeny Park, the AKC Dog Museum boasts an impressive array of art celebrating man's best friend, including paintings, drawings, sculptures and figurines. Museum is closed on Sunday and Monday. Admission for children ages 5 to 14 is only $1.00.

AQUAPORT AT MARYLAND HEIGHTS CENTER
West County

2344 McKelvey Rd.
Maryland Heights, MO 63043
314.738.2599 | www.marylandheights.com/index.aspx?page=97
Soak up the sun while floating down the Lazy River, splashing in the pool amidst sprinklers and fountains, twisting and turning down the waterslides or—if you're feeling adventurous—tackling the funnel-shaped Extreme Bowl.

BLACK MADONNA SHRINE AND GROTTOS
West County

100 Saint Josephs Hill Rd.
Pacific, MO 63069
636.938.5361 | www.franciscancaring.org/blackmadonnashri.html
A testament to what one man, in this case a polish monk, can do when he sets his mind (and heart) to it. These extraordinary grottos were built completely by hand out of natural resources. The Fransiscan Missionary Brothers offer guided tours, and self-guided tours are also an option. Admission is free.

BUTTERFLY HOUSE
West County

15193 Olive Blvd.
Chesterfield, MO 63017
636.530.0076 | www.butterflyhouse.org
Located in beautiful Faust Park, the Butterfly House offers visitors a chance to observe various species of butterflies up close in the 75 degree Conservatory. The Butterfly House is closed on Mondays and admission is free for children 2 and under.

CAROUSEL AT FAUST PARK
West County

15189 Olive Blvd.
Chesterfield, MO 63017
314.615.8383 | www.stlouisco.com/parks/carousel/carousel.htm
This whimsical carousel, created in the 1920's, has been restored to its original beauty and can be ridden for only $1.00.

CHESTERFIELD SPORTS FUSION
West County

140 Long Rd.
Chesterfield, MO 63005
636.536.6720 | www.chesterfieldsportsfusion.com
There's so much to do! Mini-golf, rock climbing, an obstacle course, dodge ball, laser tag, an arcade and a giant indoor playground make up this amazing complex. Chesterfield Sports Fusion is a perfect spot for an unforgettable birthday party.

The Best Dad/Child Activities

ENDANGERED WOLF CENTER
West County

6750 Tyson Valley Rd.
Eureka, MO, 63025-1669
636.938.5900 | www.endangeredwolfcenter.org
Visitors can observe wolves in their natural settings and learn about efforts to protect endangered wolves from extinction. Before you take the kids to the center, visit their website and play the online game WolfQuest together. Reservations are required for all tours.

KEMP AUTO MUSEUM
West County

16955 Chesterfield Airport Rd.
Chesterfield, MO 63005-1405
636.537.1718 | www.kempautomuseum.org
Housing one of the finest collections of Mercedes Benz in the world along with other rare and vintage European automobiles, dads and kids alike will be in awe. Museum is open Wednesday through Sunday, 10am to 5pm.

ST. LOUIS BALLET SCHOOL
West County

218 THF Blvd.
Chesterfield, MO 63005
636.537.1998 | www.stlouisballetschool.org
A variety of dance and music classes, including ballet, hip hop and modern dance, are offered for boys and girls of all ages. WonderDads aren't afraid to get out on the dancefloor and cut a rug with their sons and daughters, so put on your dancing shoes and take a class together.

WORLD BIRD SANCTUARY
West County

125 Bald Eagle Ridge Rd.
Valley Park, MO 63088
636.225.4390 | www.worldbirdsanctuary.org
Come experience many different species of birds (and more), including eagles, falcons and hawks. Plan to attend one of the live raptor exhibits held throughout the day. Pack a lunch and take advantage of the picnic shelters surrounded with bird feeders and birdbaths. Admission is free.

THE BEST DAD/CHILD
STORES

49

CHARM BOUTIQUE
Downtown

313 N. 11th St.
St. Louis, MO 63101
314.588.8203 | www.charm-boutique.com
Your daughter will love the chic jewelry and accessories at Charm Boutique.

CITY PET SUPPLY
Downtown

210 N. 9th St.
St. Louis, MO 63101-1417
314.436.9581 | www.citypetsupply.net
City Pet Supply offers everyday pet supplies and grooming, walking and training services along with fun social events, like the Animal House Pet Social.

GEECHI'S FLORIST
Downtown

517 Olive St.
St. Louis, MO 63101
314.621.4748
Geechi's has an incredible staff that is happy to assist in picking out and arranging the perfect bouquet for moms and daughters.

GIBBOL'S NOVELTIES & COSTUMES
Downtown

811 N. 2nd St.
St. Louis, MO 63102
314.621.3660 | www.gibbols.com
Gibbol's offers hard-to-find costumes for adults and kids along with magic tricks and other novelty items.

LEFT BANK BOOKS
Downtown

321 N. 10th St.
St. Louis, MO 63101
314.436.3049 | www.left-bank.com
Left Bank Books is a locally owned new and used bookstore; ask for Spike, the current cat-in-residence.

LEVINE HAT COMPANY
Downtown

1416 Washington Ave.
St. Louis, MO 63103
314.231.3359 | www.levinehat.com
A genuine hat shop offering every kind of hat imaginable, Levine's provides plastic head covers so there are no worries about whose head was there prior to yours.

The Best Dad/Child Stores

MACROSUN
Downtown
1310 Washington Ave.
St. Louis, MO 63103
314.421.6400 | www.macrosun.com
A fair trade marketplace, MacroSun boasts an abundance of unique jewelry, gifts, incense, rare artifacts and more.

UMA
Downtown
1100 Locust St.
St. Louis, MO 63101
314.241.9990 | www.iloveuma.com
A quirky store with a rotating stock of unique gift ideas, such as a chalk chess set or ninja shaped cookie cutters.

WASHINGTON AVE POST
Downtown
1312 Washington Ave.
St. Louis, MO 63103
314.588.0545 | www.washingtonavepost.com
A full service coffee bar and general store, Washington Ave Post has a little bit of everything.

BIG SLEEP BOOKS
Forest Park & Central West End
239 N. Euclid Ave.
St. Louis, MO 63108
314.361.6100 | www.bigsleepbooks.com
It's no mystery why this bookstore is the definitive shop for mystery books: they're all they offer.

BOWOOD FARMS
Forest Park & Central West End
4605 Olive St.
St. Louis, MO 63108
314.454.6868 | www.bowoodfarms.com
Housed in what was once an abandoned auto repair warehouse, Bowood Farms is the perfect place for all of your gardening needs.

DOLLAR GENERAL
Forest Park & Central West End
4956 Delmar Blvd.
St. Louis, MO 63108
314.454.3881 | www.dollargeneral.com
Sometimes the smallest treasures are the best, even if they're not known for their longevity; kids will love shopping for toys and knick-knacks at this popular dollar store.

GAMEZ UNLEASHED
Forest Park & Central West End
4473 Forest Park Ave.
St. Louis, MO 63108
314.533.1911 | www.gamezunleashed.com
Gamez Unleashed is a welcoming haven for gamers; the staff can advise on which games and systems you should buy or trade.

GOODWILL INDUSTRIES
Forest Park & Central West End
4140 Forest Park Ave.
St. Louis, MO 63108-2809
314.371.1296 | www.mersgoodwill.org
This second-hand shop features clothes, toys, jewelry, furniture and accessories at unbelievable prices.

LEFT BANK BOOKS
Forest Park & Central West End
399 N. Euclid
St. Louis, MO 63105
314.367.6731 | www.left-bank.com
A local treasure, this independent bookstore offers new and used books.

MARY JANE'S
Forest Park & Central West End
387 N. Euclid Ave.
St. Louis, MO 63108
314.367.8867 | www.maryjanesshoes.com
Mary Jane's boutique promises something perfect for the girls in your life, from shoes to clothing to accessories and more.

NEW MARKET HARDWARE CO
Forest Park & Central West End
4064 Laclede Ave.
St. Louis, MO 63108
314.371.1720
An old-fashioned hardware store with a knowledgeable staff, New Market Hardware is perfect for a dad and son shopping trip.

RAINBOW
Forest Park & Central West End
4946 Delmar Blvd
St. Louis, MO 63108
314.361.4805 | www.rainbowshops.com
In addition to clothes and accessories for women, Rainbow also carries clothes, shoes and accessories for boys and girls, including juniors, infants and toddlers.

The Best Dad/Child Stores

THE SILVER LADY
Forest Park & Central West End
4736 McPherson Ave.
St. Louis, MO 63108
314.367.7587 | www.thesilver-lady.com
When you're looking for silver jewelry, The Silver Lady has you covered with one-of-a-kind necklaces, pendants, rings, bracelets and more.

CARDINALS CLUBHOUSE
Grand Center & Midtown
St. Louis Union Station
1820 Market St.
St. Louis, MO 63103
314.436.3357 | www.stlouisunionstation.com — Search "Cardinals"
www.stlouisunionstation.com/go/fb/guide/store.cfm?storeID=2137028674
Dads and kids will enjoy browsing through this large selection of authentic St. Louis Cardinals merchandise and memorabilia, including collectible game-used bats and team baseballs.

THE CANDY STATION
Grand Center & Midtown
St. Louis Union Station
1820 Market St.
St. Louis, MO 63103
314.621.0221
An old fashioned candy store offering contemporary and nostalgic candies along with other goodies, kids and grown-ups alike love The Candy Station.

CARICATURES AT UNION STATION
Grand Center & Midtown
St. Louis Union Station
1820 Market St.
St. Louis, MO 63103
314.421.0988
Commemorate your day out by having a professional cartoon drawn of you and your child.

DOG ON IT
Grand Center & Midtown
St. Louis Union Station
1820 Market St.
St. Louis, MO 63103
314.588.8258
www.stlouisunionstation.com—Search Dog On It
For the dog or dog lover in your family, this boutique offers a wide range of toys and accessories.

THE FUDGERY
Grand Center & Midtown

St. Louis Union Station
1820 Market St.
St. Louis, MO 63103
314.231.1901 | www.fudgeryfudge.com

Every child remembers their first trip to The Fudgery thanks to the singing and dancing fudgemakers; go closer to closing time for great discounts.

GAMESTOP
Grand Center & Midtown

3627 Page Blvd.
St. Louis, MO 63113
314.533.8240 | www.gamestop.com

GameStop offers everything your gamer needs, including game systems, new and used games, accessories and strategy guides.

GATEWAY NEWS
Grand Center & Midtown

St. Louis Union Station
1820 Market St.
St. Louis, MO 63103
314.436.1070 | www.stlouisunionstation.com—Search Gateway News

Reminiscent of an old drugstore, Gateway News offers a little bit of everything, including newspapers and magazines from around the world.

GRAND WIG HOUSE
Grand Center & Midtown

2911 Washington Ave.
St. Louis, MO 63103
314.533.6699

Your budding fashionista will love the Grand Wig House and their selection of funky wigs, faux fur coats and unique accessories.

KIDS FOOT LOCKER
Grand Center & Midtown

3667 Page Blvd.
St. Louis, MO 63113
314.533.2567 | www.kidsfootlocker.com

Find the perfect casual and athletic shoes, including the new Jordan Retro 13, at Kids Foot Locker.

LIDS
Grand Center & Midtown

St. Louis Union Station
1820 Market St.
St. Louis, MO 63103
314.436.2720 | www.lids.com

If you're looking for matching St. Louis Blues ball caps or the latest in athletic or fashion hats, Lids has got you covered.

The Best Dad/Child Stores

LOGOS AND LABELS
Grand Center & Midtown
St. Louis Union Station
1820 Market St.
St. Louis, MO 63103
314.621.0702 | www.stlouisunionstation.com — Search Logos & Labels
Logos and Labels is the place to stop if you're looking for St. Louis-themed gifts and apparel.

PLAY & LEARN
Grand Center & Midtown
St. Louis Union Station
1820 Market St.
St. Louis, MO 63103
314.621.6266
Play & Learn offers kids the opportunity to do just that with a selection of fun and educational toys and books to choose from, including the popular Baby Einstein products.

THE ALPINE SHOP
Mid County
440 N. Kirkwood Rd.
Kirkwood, MO 63122
314.962.7715 | www.alpineshop.com
Before you head out for an outdoor adventure, stop by the Alpine Shop to make sure you've got all the gear you'll need; this huge shop covers everything from camping and kayaking to hiking and running.

ART MART
Mid County
2355 S. Hanley Rd.
Brentwood, MO 63144-1502
314.781.9999 | www.artmartstl.com
Art Mart is regarded by many as St. Louis's best art supply store, boasting over 25,000 square feet of art supplies and related items; become a fan on Facebook to receive exclusive offers.

BARNES AND NOBLE
Mid County
8871 Ladue Rd.
Ladue, MO 63124
314.862.6280 | www.barnesandnoble.com
The Ladue location of this popular bookstore offers story time every Friday at 10am.

THE BOOK HOUSE
Mid County

9719 Manchester Rd.
St. Louis, MO 63119
314.968.4491 | www.bookhousestl.com

Consisting of over 300,000 new, used, rare and unusual books, The Book House is not the most organized store in the world, but that only makes finding unexpected treasures all the more exciting.

BORDERS
Mid County

1519 S. Brentwood Blvd.
St. Louis, MO 63144
314.918.8189 | www.borders.com

Borders offers a vast supply of books, magazines, music and other multimedia along with a charming café that serves excellent coffee and smoothies.

ELECTRIC TRAIN OUTLET
Mid County

9517 Page Ave.
St. Louis, MO 63132-1523
314.428.2211 | www.electrictrainoutlet.com

If you're looking for a gift for a model train enthusiast or need to have an electric train repaired, give the folks at Electric Train Outlet a call.

THE FANTASY SHOP
Mid County

7238 Manchester Rd.
St. Louis, MO 63143
314.644.3070 | www.fantasyshoponline.com

The Fantasy Shop is home to a large collection of new and vintage comic books and games, and the staff really knows their stuff; an excellent environment for father and son bonding and arguing over who would win in a fight between Batman and Spiderman.

HOBBY LOBBY
Mid County

1215 S. Kirkwood Rd.
Kirkwood, MO 63122
314.821.1899 | www.hobbylobby.com

If you and your kids are looking for a hobby to work on together such as drawing, crafting, collecting or model building, Hobby Lobby can provide the supplies and guidance that you need.

HOBBY STATION
Mid County

301 S. Kirkwood Rd.
Kirkwood, MO 63122-6117
314.822.1927

The staff at this hobby boutique is friendly and knowledgeable, and the offerings include an extensive array of model trains, boats, cars and airplanes.

The Best Dad/Child Stores

IMAGINATION TOYS
Mid County
9737 Clayton Rd.
St. Louis, MO 63124
314.993.6288 | www.imagination-toys.com
The premier specialty toy shop in St. Louis, Imagination Toys maintains a huge selection of educational and creative toys, including new toys and classics; they also have a wide selection of games, puzzles and books.

JANIE AND JACK
Mid County
St. Louis Galleria
1451 St. Louis Galleria
Richmond Heights, MO 63117
314.725.9222 | www.janie-and-jack.com
This upscale shop offers special-occasion baby and toddler clothes; shop at the end of seasons to find the best deals.

JILLYBEAN CHILDREN'S BOUTIQUE
Mid County
9224 Clayton Rd.
Ladue, MO 63124
636.220.4221 | www.jillybeanboutique.com
Jillybean specializes in the latest designer trends in baby and children's fashions.

KANGAROO KIDS
Mid County
10030 Manchester Rd.
St. Louis, MO 63122
314.835.9200 | www.kangarookidsonline.com
This independent resale shop features great bargains on gently-used children's and maternity clothes and accessories and top-notch new items, such as strollers; this is the perfect shop for an expecting or new mother.

KIRKWOOD FARMERS' MARKET
Mid County
150 E. Argonne Dr.
Kirkwood, MO 63122
314.822.0084
www.downtownkirkwood.com/kirkwood-farmers-market.asp
This open air market in the heart of Kirkwood is home to a wide variety of vendors offering fresh produce, baked goods, meats and cheeses, homemade snacks and more; come early on a Saturday morning for the best selection.

KIRKWOOD KNITTERY
Mid County

10724 Manchester Rd.
Kirkwood, MO 63122
314.822.7222 | www.kirkwoodknittery.com

This yarn store carries everything from standard to natural and exotic yarns that you won't find anywhere else; classes are offered for knitters of all skill levels, a fun idea for dad and daughter bonding.

LASS & LADDIE
Mid County

161 W. Jefferson Ave.
Kirkwood, MO 63122-4007
314.822.1886 | www.lassandladdiehandmade.com

An independent boutique offering beautiful and unique modern and vintage handmade children's clothing at affordable prices, Lass & Laddie is the perfect place to take your son or daughter to find a one-of-a-kind outfit.

O'MALLEY'S IRISH GIFT SHOP
Mid County

2718 Sutton Boulevard
Saint Louis, MO 63143-3036
(314) 645-8779

Celebrate your Irish heritage or find the perfect gift for someone who does at this independent shop that offers first class service and authentic Irish goods such as hats, sweaters, music, jewelry and gifts.

PAINT ME POTTERY
Mid County

11215 Manchester Rd.
Kirkwood, MO 63122
314.822.7733

Bring your little artist to Paint Me Pottery, where you can choose from a huge selection of pieces to paint and decorate as creatively as you choose; a great way to spend an afternoon and perfect for birthday parties.

SPICERS
Mid County

8859 Ladue Rd.
Saint Louis, MO 63124
314.721.6026

A classic five and dime store, Spicers is full to the brim with random toys, party favors, children's costumes and other assorted items; Spicers is particularly fascinating during the holiday seasons and a great place to search for unique gifts and decorations.

The Best Dad/Child Stores

STRASBURG CHILDREN
Mid County

26 The Blvd. St. Louis
Richmond Heights, MO 63117
314.863.6840 | www.strasburgchildren.com
When you're looking for the finest in special occasion and seasonal apparel for your son or daughter, Strasburg Children is the place to start; the attention to detail given to these timeless classics is second to none.

ANIMAGINATION
North County

St. Louis Mills Mall
5555 St. Louis Mills Blvd.
Hazelwood, MO 63042
314.227.5757
You can explore the popular worlds of anime, gaming and fantasy with your son or daughter at this unique shop.

BARNES AND NOBLE
North County

13995 New Halls Ferry Rd.
Florissant, MO 63033
314.830.3550 | www.barnesandnoble.com
This popular bookstore chain offers a large selection of new books, magazines, music, DVDs and other media; there's lots of space to sprawl out and preview before you buy, preferably with a cup of coffee or hot chocolate from the in-store café.

THE BOEING STORE
North County

5900 N. Lindbergh Blvd.
Hazelwood, MO 63042
314.233.2222 | www.boeingstore.com
The Boeing Store features products celebrating and commemorating the Boeing Company's many achievements along with inventive toys, kits and puzzles for your inquisitive engineer in training; featured items include Blue Angels collectibles.

BOOKS-A-MILLION
North County

St. Louis Mills Mall
5555 St. Louis Mills Blvd.
Hazelwood, MO 63042
314.227.5263 | www.booksamillion.com
The third largest book retailer in the nation, Books-A-Million located in the St. Louis Mills Mall provides an expansive selection of books and magazines, including bargain books and children's selections.

CABELA'S
North County

St. Louis Mills Mall
5555 St. Louis Mills Blvd.
Hazelwood, MO 63042
314.225.0100 | www.cabelas.com

A well-respected outdoors person's paradise, Cabela's has a vast array of fishing, hunting and camping gear and casual sporting attire.

GLIDESCOPE RADIO CONTROL AIRCRAFT
North County

160 Jamestown Mall
Florissant, MO 63034
314.438.0505 | www.glidescoperc.com

If you or your child is an RC enthusiast, you'll find what you're looking for at Glidescope, which carries everything from diecast models, toys and games to remote control planes, helicopters and cars.

JUSTICE
North County

St. Louis Mills Mall
5555 St. Louis Mills Blvd.
Hazelwood, MO 63042
314.227.5446 | www.shopjustice.com

The kind of shop that your daughter will love, Justice carries all of the latest fashions for girls, including funky tees and skinny jeans.

KIDS AGAIN
North County

630 N. Lindbergh, Hwy. 67
Florissant, MO 63031
314.839.8805 | www.kidsagainstl.com

A friendly and affordable resale shop, the family-owned and operated Kids Again buys and sells quality children and maternity items and includes a play area for the kids.

LAGOONAMAGOO TOYS
North County

St. Louis Mills Mall
5555 St. Louis Mills Blvd.
Hazelwood, MO 63042
314.227.5335 | happyupinc.com

Featuring unique and creative toys, Lagoonamagoo takes playing very seriously and goes out of its way to equip your kids with the best tools of the trade; popular selections include deluxe art kits and imaginative building blocks sets.

The Best Dad/Child Stores

MALAWI AQUATICS INTERNATIONAL
North County
11619 W. Florissant Blvd.
St. Louis, MO 63033
314.830.6460 | www.malawi-aquatics.com
Going way beyond the average goldfish, Malawi Aquatics specializes in African Cichlids; the staff delights in welcoming and educating fish enthusiasts young and old.

NAGLE'S
North County
19 Patterson Plz.
Florissant, MO 63031
314.838.4444
This popular variety store has been delighting children and adults for years with their selection of candy, toys and novelty items.

ONCE UPON A CHILD
North County
8 Paddock Hills Plz.
Florissant, MO 63033
314.831.2255 | www.onceuponachildcrevecoeur.com
Once Upon a Child offers new and gently-used children's clothes, toys, books and more; they also buy the clothes, toys, furniture and equipment that your kids have outgrown.

SKECHERS USA
North County
St. Louis Mills Mall
5555 St. Louis Mills Blvd.
Hazelwood, MO 63042
314.227.5868 | www.skechers.com
The coolest shoes for adults and kids, from athletic and casual to dress, can be found at Skechers.

SPORTS AUTHORITY
North County
11982 Saint Charles Rock Rd.
Bridgeton, MO 63044
314.739.1344 | www.sportsauthority.com
Sports Authority sells all the major brands in sporting goods and also provides such services as bike repair, ice skate sharpening, and hunting and fishing licenses.

TOYS 'R' US
North County

10895 W. Florissant Ave.
Calverton Park, MO 63136
314.521.0666 | www.toysrus.com

If it's a toy, you'll find it at Toys 'R' Us; all of your kid's favorites, from Ben 10 to Hannah Montana to Iron Man, are well-represented in aisle upon aisle of toys.

2ND STREET BIKE STOP CAFÉ
St. Charles

1325 N. 2nd St.
St. Charles, MO 63301
636.724.9900 | www.2ndstreetbikestopcafe.com

2nd Street Bike Stop Café is a brilliant combination of coffee house and bike shop that allows you to enjoy a healthy breakfast or lunch while waiting for your bike to be repaired; new and used bikes and accessories are available to buy.

A POCKETFUL OF TOYS
St. Charles

9987 Winghaven Blvd.
O'Fallon, MO 63368
636.561.3222

This independent toy retailer includes a selection of classic and vintage toys along with crafting kits, puzzles and a slew of games perfect for family game night.

ANIMAL CRACKERS
St. Charles

343 Winding Woods Center
O'Fallon, MO 63366
636.474.3647 | www.animalcrackersofallonmo.blogspot.com

Every kid wants their pet to be a healthy pet, so you'll be a hero for checking out the selection of dog and cat health food at Animal Crackers; pets are always welcome.

BARNES AND NOBLE
St. Charles

320 Mid Rivers Center Dr.
St Peters, MO 63376
636.278.1118 | www.barnesandnoble.com

In addition to the countless new books and other media expected from Barnes and Noble, a children's story time is scheduled every Saturday.

The Best Dad/Child Stores

BASS PRO SHOPS
SPORTSMAN'S WAREHOUSE St. Charles
1365 S. 5th St.
St. Charles, MO 63301
636.688.2500 | www.basspro.com/homepage.html
Headquartered in Springfield, MO, Bass Pro Shop is a popular one-stop shop for everything outdoors; Saturdays are family days at the Sportsman's Warehouse and feature special guests and activities.

BOOKMARK BOOK SHOPS St. Charles
520 S. 5th St.
St. Charles, MO 63301
636.946.4926
Bookmark specializes in educational books and caters to teachers and parents; the store has a play area for children.

BORDERS St. Charles
1320 Mid Rivers Mall
St. Peters, MO 63376
636.278.5000 | www.borders.com
In addition to the usual extensive selection of books, movies and music, this store features singing baristas in the café, family game nights and other special events.

DICK'S SPORTING GOODS St. Charles
1600 Mid Rivers Mall
St. Peters, MO 63376
636.278.5050 | www.dickssportinggoods.com
Dick's is a perfect place to get equipped before taking to the field, running the course or tackling the great outdoors with your son or daughter.

FAMILY CHRISTIAN STORE St. Charles
167 Mid Rivers Mall Dr.
St. Peters, MO 63376
636.278.2895 | www.familychristian.com
Family Christian Store offers age-appropriate books, Bibles, music, apparel and videos, including the popular VeggieTales series.

THE FANTASY SHOP St. Charles
2426 W. Clay St.
St. Charles, MO 63301
636.947.8330 | www.fantasyshoponline.com
Dads and kids can browse through new and vintage comics at The Fantasy Shop and debate the merits of heroes of years past compared to those of today.

MAIN STREET BOOKS
St. Charles
307 S. Main St.
St. Charles, MO 63301
636.949.0105 | www.mainstreetbooks.net
Located in historic St. Charles, Main Street Books is a quaint and cozy independent bookstore; the owner is usually available and happy to chat with you and your kids about the hottest new releases and classics.

NATIVE TRADITIONS
St. Charles
310 S. Main St.
St. Charles, MO 63301
636.947.0170
This Native American gallery features jewelry, sculptures and other unique gift ideas that would make stunning birthday presents.

PUDDLE DUCKS
St. Charles
21 Meadows Circle Dr. Ste. 316
Lake St. Louis, MO 63367
636.561.5153 | www.puddleducksonline.com
This small boutique offers gifts, baby clothes, quality toys and books at very reasonable prices; Puddle Ducks is a perfect stop for dads looking to spoil their daughters.

SOCCER MASTER
St. Charles
6115 Mid Rivers Mall Dr. & Hwy. N
St. Peters, MO 63376
636.397.7627 | www.soccermaster.com
Soccer Master does one thing and does it well, catering to those in the market for soccer shoes, uniforms or equipment.

TOYS "R" US
St. Charles
5821 Sue Mandy Dr.
St. Peters, MO 63376
636.397.5000 | www.toysrus.com
Look no further than Toys "R" Us for a vast selection of the most popular toys, video games and related items on the market today.

ALL ALONG PRESS
Soulard & Cherokee Street
2712 Cherokee St.
St. Louis, MO 63104
314.827.6185 | www.allalongpress.com
A co-op print shop specializing in letterpress and screen printing, All Along Press offers printmaking facilities to the public and hosts various classes and workshops in addition to operating a store that sells handmade books, cards and stationary and posters; perfect for older kids interested in book arts.

The Best Dad/Child Stores

CRANKY YELLOW
Soulard & Cherokee Street
2847 Cherokee St.
St. Louis, MO 63118
314.773.4499 | www.crankyyellow.com
Cranky Yellow may not be considered a "kid's store" per se, but for the hip dad looking to pass on his appreciation of indy art and handmade and vintage goods, it's the perfect spot for some father/child bonding.

FIRECRACKER PRESS
Soulard & Cherokee Street
2838 Cherokee St.
St. Louis, MO 63118
314.776.7271 | www.firecrackerpress.com
Firecracker Press specializes in funky one-of-a-kind posters that would make a great gift for the cool kid in your life.

HAMMOND'S ANTIQUES & BOOKS
Soulard & Cherokee Street
1939 Cherokee St.
St. Louis, MO 63118-3251
314.776.4737 | hammondsbooks.net
Hammonds feels like a giant house filled to the brim with used, rare and collectible books and is a perfect way to spend a rainy day; if you're looking for a particular book, call ahead and they'll find it for you.

PANORAMA FOLK ART
Soulard & Cherokee Street
1925 Cherokee St.
St. Louis, MO 63118
314.772.8007 | www.panoramafolkart.com
For a unique decorative gift that will impress both your family and friends, check out Panorama's handmade folk art and paintings; a perfect environment for the budding artist.

PASTE
Soulard & Cherokee Street
1009 Russell Blvd.
St. Louis, MO 63104
314.577.6930 | pastecrafts.com
An arts and crafts supply store that also carries a selection of affordable, handmade products from local artists, Paste is quickly becoming the city destination for all things arts and crafts; check out their schedule of classes for something fun to do together.

THE PURPLE COW
Soulard & Cherokee Street

2010 Cherokee St.
St. Louis, MO 63118
314.771.9400

A most unusual antique shop with character to spare, The Purple Cow specializes in random items and an art-deco feel; of particular interest may be the vintage postcards, signs and sports memorabilia.

RETRO 101 & CHERRY BOMB VINTAGE
Soulard & Cherokee Street

2303 Cherokee St.
St. Louis, MO 63118
314.762.9722 | www.retro-101.com

Whether your kids want to stock their dress-up box or find something truly hip and retro so they can strut their style, Retro 101 & Cherry Bomb Vintage fits the bill with their impressive selection of kitschy clothes and other funky merchandise.

SOULARD FARMERS MARKET
Soulard & Cherokee Street

730 Carroll St.
St. Louis, MO 63104
314.622.4180 | www.stlouis.missouri.org/citygov/soulardmarket

Shopping in this open air market on a Saturday morning is fun for the whole family, and the huge selection of vendors offering everything from fresh produce, flowers and spices to unique gifts and jewelry will make the trip a pleasure as opposed to a chore.

STL-STYLE
Soulard & Cherokee Street

3159 Cherokee St.
St. Louis, MO 63118
314.494.7763 | www.stl-style.com

St. Louis is an idiosyncratic town, and the folks at STL-Style have embraced it, creating colorful St. Louis-themed clothes and items that celebrate everything that makes St. Louis the place that it is; see if you can find a tee shirt representing your neighborhood.

ALL AMERICAN COLLECTIBLES
South City

6933 Hampton Ave.
St Louis, MO 63109-4107
314.352.7700 | www.aac-mo.com

For everything pop culture, from comic books to trading cards to toys, All American Collectibles is a place where dads can act like kids, too.

The Best Dad/Child Stores

CRM HOBBIES
South City

5101 Eichelberger St.
St. Louis, MO 63109-3236
314.832.4840 | www.crmhobbies.com

Dads and sons can find all the supplies they need to undertake a project together, like building a model tank or aircraft.

CARONDELET BAKERY
South City

7726 Virginia Ave.
St. Louis, MO 63111
314.638.3519 | www.carondeletbakery.com

St. Louis's oldest bakery is closed on Sundays and Mondays, but on any other day of the week you can find them doling out inventive and delicious custom decorated cakes for any occasion.

DUNAWAY BOOKS
South City

3111 S. Grand Blvd.
St. Louis, MO 63118
314.771.7150 | www.dunawaybooks.com

A clean, well-organized used book store that's easy to navigate, Dunaway Books offers a diverse selection and fair prices; includes a section of children's books.

FYE
South City

3801 Hampton Ave.
St. Louis, MO 63109
314.353.5551 | www.fye.com

If you're looking for a particular CD or DVD for yourself or your child, chances are good that FYE will have it.

JANINE'S TOTES TOTS TOILE
South City

2924 S. Grand Blvd.
St. Louis, MO 63118
314.664.3742 | www.janines.org/aboutus.html

Your daughter will love Janine's and all of the fun and glamorous items she has to offer, including clothes, jewelry and accessories.

KNITORIOUS
South City

3268 Watson Rd.
St. Louis, MO 63139-2459
314.646.8276 | www.knitorious.com

Knitting has never been more popular and Knitorious could be considered the mecca of knitting; every kind of yarn you can imagine and all of the supplies you could ever need are here, along with helpful and friendly staff to help you get started.

THE RECORD EXCHANGE
South City

5320 Hampton Ave.
St. Louis, MO 63109
314.832.2249 | www.recordexchangestl.com

It's easy to be overwhelmed by The Record Exchange's 10,000 square feet of music and memorabilia, but it's worth any anxiety to have such an amazing and diverse collection of CDs and vinyl at your fingertips.

TFA
South City

3229 Morganford Rd.
St. Louis, MO 63116-1831
314.865.1552 | www.tfa50s.com

Give TFA's vintage furniture and knick-knacks a try; your kids will love helping you pick out your new couch and you'll enjoy the feeling of nostalgia.

TOWER GROVE FARMERS MARKET & BAZAAR
South City

Tower Grove Park
Northwest Dr. & Central Cross Dr.
St. Louis, MO 63139
www.tgmarket.org

Come spend a morning shopping for the freshest local produce and other foods; maybe the whole family would enjoy getting their early on Saturday morning and participating in the free yoga classes.

ABRA-KID-ABRA
South County

126 Crestwood Plaza
Crestwood, MO 63126
314.961.6912 | www.abrakid.com

Prepare to be amazed by Abra-Kid-Abra's supply of magic and circus tricks and accessories; even better, let the kids really get in on the act at one of their camps or classes.

APPLE OF YOUR EYE
South County

20 N. Gore Ave.
St. Louis, MO 63119-2355
314.968.9698 | www.appleofyoureyegifts.com

You'll be hailed as a genius on Mother's Day when you bring the kids to pick out the perfect personalized gift for mom.

The Best Dad/Child Stores

BAKED GOODS POTTERY
South County
11557 Gravois Rd.
St. Louis, MO 63126
314.842.0110 | www.bakedgoodspottery.com
Pick out your favorite piece of unfinished pottery and create your masterpiece with the help of the friendly staff.

BARNES AND NOBLE
South County
9618 Watson Rd.
St. Louis, MO 63126
314.843.9480
721 Gravois Rd.
Fenton, MO 63026
636.326.4619 | www.barnesandnoble.com
This popular bookstore chain offers a large selection of new books, magazines, music, DVDs and other media, with coffee and comfy chairs to boot; check website for kids story time schedule.

BFF (BEST FRIEND FUREVER) RESCUE
South County
Fenton, MO 63026
636.326.9742 | www.bffrescue.net
Be a household hero when you come home with the newest member of the family, an adorable rescued puppy.

BORDERS
South County
10990 Sunset Hills Plz.
Sunset Hills, MO 63127
314.909.0300
25 S. County Centerway
St. Louis, MO 63129
414.892.1700 | www.borders.com
In addition to the expected selection of books, Borders also boasts a large Local Interest section full of great books (like this one).

CHECKERED FLAG HOBBY COUNTRY
South County
4491 Lemay Ferry Rd.
St. Louis, MO 63129-1757
314.892.5353 | www.cfhobby.com
This hobby center appeals to both brothers and sisters with a wide variety of model kits, dollhouses, radio controlled cars, rockets and craft supplies.

CIRCLE OF KNOWLEDGE
South County

10980 Sunset Hills Plz.
Sunset Hills, MO 63127
314.821.5150 | www.circleofknowledge.com
An exciting and inventive toy store that offers only the highest quality toys, the kind that can be passed down from older siblings to younger.

INFINITY SKATE SHOP
South County

5528 S. Lindbergh Blvd.
St. Louis, MO 63123
314.843.1989 | www.infinityskateshop.com
For the skater in the family, this is the perfect spot for affordable boards and gear; don't worry, they also sell helmets and protective pads.

LADY BUG BEADS
South County

7616 Big Bend Blvd.
St. Louis, MO 63119-2106
314.644.6140 | www.ladybugbeads.net
Your little girl will love browsing through this massive selection of beads and turning them into one-of-a-kind necklaces and bracelets for herself and, of course, for you.

MICRO ENGINEERING COMPANY
South County

1120 Eagle Rd.
Fenton, MO 63026-4507
636.349.1112 | www.microengineering.biz
Some things never go out of style, like fathers working with their sons on model railroads; get everything you need at Micro Engineering Company.

MINIATURE MARKET
South County

924 S. Hwy. Dr.
Fenton, MO 63026
1.877.326.4429 | www.miniaturemarket.com
If your son enjoys Dungeons & Dragons or Magic the Gathering, you'll find everything you need to play along at Miniature Market.

READING HABITAT
South County

6035 Telegraph Rd.
Saint Louis, MO 63129
314.293.2400 | www.readinghabitat.com
Reading Habitat can help your child foster a love of reading; plus, they have Starbucks coffee and free Wi-Fi available for parents.

The Best Dad/Child Stores

SLACKERS
South County

18 S. County Center Way
St. Louis, MO 63129-1007
314.845.5155 | www.slackers.com
"Slackers" is a good thing, at least when you're talking about this hook-up for new and used video games, systems, CDs and DVDs.

YUCANDU
South County

20 Allen Ave.
Webster Groves, MO 63119
314.963.4400 | www.yucandu.com
Bring your artist with you to Yucandu and admire their handiwork as they create works of art with mosaic, paint, decoupage and more.

BLOOMS IN THE LOOP FLORIST
University City

6346 Delmar Blvd.
St. Louis, MO 63130
314.725.8080 | www.bloomsintheloop.com
Excellent service makes this a wonderful choice for saying "I love you" with flowers.

CHINA TOWN MARKET
University City

8150 Olive Blvd.
St. Louis, MO 63130
314.432.3972
Take the little ones shopping at this Asian food market and surprise mom with an authentic home-cooked meal.

CITY SPROUTS
University City

6303 Delmar Blvd.
St. Louis, MO
314.726.9611 | www.citysprouts.com
Kids deserve cool clothes and gear, and City Sprouts knows cool.

CRAFT ALLIANCE
University City

6640 Delmar Blvd.
St. Louis, MO 63130
314.725.1177 | www.craftalliance.org
Sign up for a parent/child art class or shop for some unique hand-made gifts.

GAME CRAZY
University City
6662 Delmar Blvd.
St. Louis, MO 63130
314.721.2925 | www.gamecrazy.com
The store always has the latest and greatest in in gaming systems and more.

HEADZ & THREADZ
University City
6662 Delmar Blvd.
St. Louis, MO 63130
314.863.2695 | www.headznthreadz.com
You can buy an off-the-shelf hat, but why not go all the way and have one custom embroidered or screen printed while you're there?

MISS M'S CANDY BOUTIQUE
University City
6193 Delmar Blvd.
St. Louis, MO 63130
314.721.7000 | www.missmscandy.com
Why just feel like a kid in a candy shop when you can be a kid in a candy shop? Miss M's offers the best in contemporary and nostalgic candies and gifts.

PHOENIX RISING
University City
6331 Delmar Blvd.
St. Louis, MO 63130
314.862.0609 | www.shopphoenixrising.com
When you need a tin of bandages that look like bacon or funky socks, you should automatically head to Phoenix Rising.

STAR CLIPPER
University City
6392 Delmar Blvd.
St. Louis, MO 63130
314.725.9110 | www.starclipper.com
Get your young son hooked on the adventures of Wolverine or Superman at Star Clipper, which features toys and collectibles in addition to comic books and graphic novels.

SUBTERRANEAN BOOKS
University City
6275 Delmar Blvd.
Saint Louis, MO 63130
314.862.6100 | www.subbooks.com
If you don't know what to get your favorite reader, the staff at Subterranean Books will.

The Best Dad/Child Stores

SUPER 9
University City
8008 Olive Blvd.
St. Louis, MO 63130
314.997.8200
Bring the kids to this eclectic discount store for a shopping adventure.

TIMELESS AUTHENTIC GARMENTS (TAG)
University City
6314 Delmar Blvd.
St. Louis, MO 63130
314.721.1370
It's only a matter of time before your kids start telling you that you have no fashion sense; when they do, head to TAG for stylish vintage duds.

TRAINS LTD
University City
8151 Delmar Blvd.
University City, MO 63130-3729
314.721.2939 | www.trains-ltd.com
Nearly every child goes through a Thomas the Tank Engine stage; when yours does, Trains LTD will have your back by stocking the complete line of Thomas wooden trains.

VINTAGE VINYL
University City
6610 Delmar Blvd.
St. Louis, MO 63130
314.721.4096 | www.vintagevinyl.com
No matter what you're looking for, Vintage Vinyl will either have it or get it (and they won't laugh when you ask them to track down an obscure release by The Wiggles).

YOUR POT'S DESIRE
University City
7700 Delmar Blvd.
St. Louis, MO 63130
314.601.3982 | www.yourpotsdesire.com
All moms know that handmade gifts are the best; you can really impress by spending an afternoon with your son or daughter at Your Pot's Desire and painting the perfect pottery gift.

ARCHIVER'S
West County
214 Chesterfield Mall
Chesterfield, MO 63017-4811
636.530.7027 | www.archiversonline.info
Mom will love it when the kids give her a scrapbook courtesy of Archiver's.

BARNES AND NOBLE
West County

1600 Clarkson Rd.
Chesterfield, MO 63017
636.536.9636
113 West County Center
Des Peres, MO 63131
314.835.9980 | www.barnesandnoble.com
Relax with a cup of coffee and a book while the little ones enjoy story time. Check the website for times.

BOOK RACK
West County

14560 Manchester Rd. Ste. 14
Ballwin, MO 63011
636.394.1233 | www.bookrack-stl.com
This used book store is happy to accommodate special requests.

BORDERS
West County

15355A Manchester Rd.
Ballwin, MO 63011
636.230.2992
11745 Olive Blvd.
Creve Coeur, MO 63141
314.432.3575
2040 Chesterfield Mall
Chesterfield, MO 63017
636.536.1779 | www.borders.com
These locations offer large kids and young adult sections along with weekly special events.

BRIGHT IDEA TOYS LLC
West County

13476 Clayton Rd.
St. Louis, MO 63131-1006
314.205.8555
You'll find a wide selection of unique electronic and educational toys guaranteed to please.

CHOCOLATE SOUP
West County

13456 Clayton Rd.
St. Louis, MO 63131-1006
314.576.1221
If it's not an adorable children's outfit, it doesn't belong at Chocolate Soup.

The Best Dad/Child Stores

CRAZY 8
West County

262 Chesterfield Mall
Chesterfield, MO 63017-4811
636.536.0940 | www.crazy8.com
Outfit your kids in style with clothes from Crazy 8.

DESIGNS IN MOTION
West County

700 Spirit Of Saint Louis Blvd.
Chesterfield, MO 63005-1025
636.519.1011 | www.designsinm.com
Designs in Motion carries only the highest quality diecast collectibles and can get your son started on a lifelong hobby.

HOBBYTOWN USA
West County

15037 Manchester Rd.
Ballwin, MO 63011-4626
636.394.0177 | www.hobbytown.com
Discover a new indoor or outdoor hobby to enjoy with your kids at Hobbytown USA.

POTTERY BARN KIDS
West County

265 Chesterfield Mall
Chesterfield, MO 63017-4810
636.536.3823 | www.potterybarnkids.com
Decorate your child's room with styles from Pottery Barn Kids and you'll know you made a good choice.

SPORTS FAN ATTIC
West County

69 W. County Ctr.
Des Peres, MO 63131-3701
314.821.9292 | www.sportsfanattic.bzfs.com
Stop by prior to your camping adventure and you can't go wrong.

THE GOLDEN HORSESHOE TACK SHOP
West County

319 N. Central Ave.
Eureka, MO 63025-1827
636.938.4309
www.facebook.com/pages/Golden-Horseshoe-Tack-Shop/69766447230
Whether you have an equestrian on your hands or just a horse lover, you'll find something worthwhile at this independent tack shop.

TOY TYME
West County

146 Chesterfield Valley Dr.
Chesterfield, MO 63005-1161
636.532.9696 | www.toytyme.com
Featuring classic toys and games, this is St. Louis's largest specialty toy store.

UNIQUE TOY & GAME
West County

15531 Manchester Rd.
Ballwin, MO 63011
636.227.2400 | www.uniquetoyandgame.com
Every Tuesday is Grandparent's Day at this specialty toy store; tell grandpa to take the kids for a 10% discount.

VARIETEES
West County

60 Meramec Valley Plz.
Valley Park, MO 63088
636.225.2473 | www.vbirdshop.com
Would your kids like a pet bird? Does Polly want a cracker?

WHITTLE SHORTLINE RAILROAD
West County

24 Front St.
Valley Park, MO 63088-1602
636.861.3334 | www.woodentrain.com
The classics never go out of style; you'll enjoy bonding with your son over these classic wooden trains.

THE BEST DAD/CHILD
OUTDOOR PARKS & RECREATION

CITY GARDEN
Downtown
S. 8th St & Market St.
St. Louis, MO 63101
314.241.3337 | www.citygardenstl.org
Kid will love splashing around in the fountain and enjoy the amazing sculptures dotting the City Garden landscape; enjoy a picnic on a sunny spring day, or stop by the Terrace View café for lunch or dinner.

THE CONFLUENCE
Downtown
1533 Washington Ave.
St. Louis, MO 63103
314.436.1324 | www.confluencegreenway.org
The Confluence consists of 200 square miles of conservation, recreation and heritage attractions along the Mississippi, Missouri and Illinois Rivers. There are many possibilities and opportunities to make a day out of hiking, biking, hunting, birdwatching or even island hopping; follow up your chosen adventure with dinner downtown at the Old Spaghetti Factory.

ECKERT'S COUNTRY STORE AND FARMS
Downtown
951 Green Mount Rd.
Belleville, IL 62220
618.233.0513 | www.eckerts.com
Eckert's famous farm is only 25 minutes across the river from Downtown St. Louis; enjoy apple and pumpkin picking, an old fashioned country store and special events throughout the year. Go in the spring for the choicest selection of apples and the fall for quality pumpkins just waiting to be carved.

LUCAS GARDEN PARK
Downtown
1234 Washington Ave.
St. Louis, MO 63103
314.421.1023
www.stlouis.missouri.org/citygov/parks/parks_div/lucas.html
Stop by on a summer day and enjoy a relaxing picnic by the pond after watching your kids climb on the turtle statue and play on the playgrounds.

SERRA SCULPTURE PARK
Downtown
10th, 11th, Market and Chestnut St.
St. Louis, MO 63101
www.stlouis.missouri.org/citygov/parks/parks_div/serra.html
This downtown park is famous for "Twain," a divisive sculpture by artist Richard Serra consisting of 8 slabs of steel designed to be looked through. Some people love it and others hate it, but it's definitely worth checking out.

The Best Dad/Child Outdoor Parks & Recreation

FOREST PARK
Forest Park & Central West End
5595 Grand Dr.
St. Louis, MO 63112
314.289.5300 | www.stlouis.missouri.org/citygov/parks/forestpark
The heart of the city, Forest Park is home to the St. Louis Zoo, the St. Louis Art Museum and much, much more. There's so much to do, it's best to make plans to come back often or at the very least dedicate a whole day. This vast park offers lots of options for family fun, from biking together to enjoying a meal on the outdoor patio of the Boathouse. Forest Park knows no season – Catch a show in the free seats at the Muny on a starry summer night or sled down Art Hill in the winter.

THE GREAT FOREST PARK BALLOON RACE
Forest Park & Central West End
Forest Park
St. Louis, MO 63112
www.greatforestparkballoonrace.com
The 39th annual hot air balloon race will be held in September, 2011. Watch as a host of hot air balloons take to the skies and keep an eye out for the Energizer Bunny "hare" balloon. Bring the kids down the night before the race for the balloon glow and navigate through a field of lit up balloons. The Balloon Race is free to attend; get there early to avoid a parking struggle.

ST. STEPHEN'S PLAYGROUND
Forest Park & Central West End
Olive St. & Pendleton Ave.
St. Louis, MO 63108-3025
This new playground in the Central West End boasts swings, a twisty slide, monkey bars and more, and is a great place to stop and expend some energy while exploring all that the Central West End has to offer. Grab a light snack with your daughter at nearby Crepes Etc. before you go.

SHAKESPEARE FESTIVAL OF ST. LOUIS
Forest Park & Central West End
462 N. Taylor Ave., Suite 202
St. Louis, MO 63108
314.531.9800 | www.shakespearefestivalstlouis.org
Held in beautiful Forest Park in May and June, the Shakespeare Festival offers visitors the opportunity to enjoy classic drama under the stars. Prior to main stage performances is The Green Show, a showcase of local artists and entertainers. Concessions are available and admission is free.

TURTLE PLAYGROUND
Forest Park & Central West End

South end of Forest Park
Oakland and Tamm Ave.
St. Louis, MO 63112
www.stlouis.missouri.org/citygov/parks/forestpark/turtle.html

Nestled in Forest Park, Turtle Playground is fast becoming one of St. Louis's most popular playgrounds. You and your kids will have a great time climbing on and around the three large and four small turtle sculptures before setting out to explore the rest of Forest Park.

COMPTON HILL RESERVOIR PARK
Grand Center & Midtown

1800 Compton Hill Pl.
St. Louis, MO 63104
www.stlouis.missouri.org/citygov/parks/parks_div/compton.html

Located to the south of Grand Center, Compton Hill Reservoir Park is home to the Compton Hill Water Tower, a 180-ft. symbol of local pride and identity. The park, which is listed on the National Registry of Historic Places, is also home to what was once the city's principal water reservoir and the statue The Naked Truth. A perfect spot for a picnic and a summer stroll, the park also includes a playground and decorative fountain.

DANCING IN THE STREET FESTIVAL
Grand Center & Midtown

Grand Center
3526 Washington Ave. #2
St. Louis, MO 63103
314.533.8825

Every September Grand Center celebrates the start of the fall arts season with this free event consisting of four outdoor stages and hundreds of dancers of all ages and styles. Local and national dancers and troupes are represented, and there are sure to be some surprise appearances. In past years, Radio Disney's Dance Team has shown up to teach kids the steps to the latest Hannah Montana dance crazes.

FAIRGROUND PARK
Grand Center & Midtown

3740 Kossuth Ave.
St. Louis, MO 63107
www.stlouis.missouri.org/citygov/parks/parks_div/fairground.html

Located just north of Grand Center in the Fairground neighborhood, Fairground Park was originally created as a home for the popular St. Louis Fair, an annual event of epic proportions. In fact, some of the old structures hearkening back to the fair's glory days can still be found in the park today. Fairgrounds Park currently includes a playground, a stocked lake for fishing, a skating rink and multiple sports fields and courts.

The Best Dad/Child Outdoor Parks & Recreation

STRAUSS PARK
Grand Center & Midtown
Washington & N. Grand Blvd.
St. Louis, MO 63103

Strauss Park is home to two popular sculptures, Earth Rabbit and After Hours, and is a wonderful stop on any tour of Grand Center. During the summer season the park occasionally hosts themed movie nights in conjunction with Front Yard Features, giving you the opportunity to replace a typical trip to the cinema with an unforgettable experience under the stars.

TANDY PARK
Grand Center & Midtown
2601 Billups Ave.
St. Louis, MO 63113
314.652.5131

Tandy Park is home to the Tandy Recreation Center, which features a gymnasium, swimming pool, game room and workout room. The park itself includes a playground, tennis courts (where Arthur Ashe once played), basketball and volleyball courts, a football field and a skating rink.

DEMUN PARK
Mid County
810 DeMun Ave.
Clayton, MO 63105
314.290.8464

DeMun is a small, gated park nestled amongst the bevy of shops and restaurants in Clayton that earns bonus points for having an excellent coffee shop next door. This is a perfect park for younger children since it contains two small playgrounds, one of which is specifically intended for toddlers.

KIRKWOOD PARK
Mid County
201 W. Adams Ave.
Kirkwood, MO 63122
www.ci.kirkwood.mo.us

Kirkwood's premier park, this 92-acre site is home to many attractions, including an outdoor amphitheater and spray fountain. Start a summer tradition and reserve a pavilion and barbeque burgers and hot dogs, or cool down in the aquatic center. The fireworks display on the 4th of July is always popular, as are concerts in the summer and the Greentree Festival in September.

OAK KNOLL PARK
Mid County
987 S. Big Bend Blvd.
Clayton, MO 63105

Oak Knoll is Clayton's second largest park. Known for its relaxing, scenic appeal, the park is the perfect spot for taking family photos or enjoying a picnic on a spring day. Also, free concerts are scheduled the fourth Sunday of each month, June through September. Bring the family and a blanket or lawn chairs and enjoy a peaceful evening out.

POWDER VALLEY CONSERVATION NATURE CENTER

Mid County

11715 Cragwold Rd.
St. Louis, MO 63122
314.301.1500 | www.mdc.mo.gov/regions/st-louis/powder-valley

Hike the trails through the lush oak-hickory forest and spend some time in the nature center viewing interactive exhibits and learning about Missouri's native wildlife. Be sure to check out the 3,000 gallon aquarium, live snake cages and other interactive exhibits tailored specifically to kids. The nature center is closed on Sundays and Mondays.

SHAW PARK

Mid County

111 South Brentwood Blvd.
Clayton, MO 63105
314.290.8501 | www.ci.clayton.mo.us/index.aspx?location=541

Located in the heart of Clayton, Shaw Park is home to an extensive aquatic center that includes a diving pool and a splash pool for the kids, an outdoor skating rink, various ball fields and courts and impressive gardens that are perfect for strolling through hand-in-hand with your son or daughter. There are plenty of available pavilions and grills, making it a perfect picnic spot.

BELLA FONTAINE PARK

North County

9565 Bellefontaine Rd.
St. Louis, MO 63137
www.stlouisco.com/parks/bella.html

Bella Fontaine Park features walking trails, tennis and basketball courts, playgrounds, a stocked lake for fishing and a top-notch softball complex.

CASTLEPOINT PARK

North County

2465 Baroness Dr.
St. Louis, MO 63136
www.stlouisco.com/parks/castlepoint.html

Kids will enjoy a trip to Castlepoint Park with its modern playground, basketball courts and a spray fountain to run through on hot summer days. For a special treat, visit the Whistle Stop, an old fashioned frozen custard shop in the historic Ferguson Train Depot and area favorite.

The Best Dad/Child Outdoor Parks & Recreation

EAGLE DAYS AT THE OLD CHAIN OF ROCKS BRIDGE
North County

10950 Riverview Dr.
St. Louis, MO 63137
573.751.4115 ext. 3289
www.mdc.mo.gov/discover-nature/programs/eagle-days
Spanning the Mississippi River, the Old Chain of Rocks Bridge is one of the world's longest bike and pedestrian bridges. Bring your bikes any time and enjoy a ride in the fresh air, or come for Eagle Days, a free annual public program that gives you and your kids a chance to watch eagles take flight and learn about them up close.

ENDICOTT PARK
North County

2950 Endicott Ave.
St. Louis, MO 63114
www.stlouisco.com/parks/endicott.html
At Endicott Park dads can challenge their kids to a round of disc golf, or vice versa. Afterwards, kids can climb around on the playground (or vice versa).

SIOUX PASSAGE
North County

17930 Old Jamestown Rd.
Florissant, MO 63034
www.stlouisco.com/parks/sioux.html
Sioux Passage offers lots of fun activities in the summer and spring with a disc golf course, playgrounds, fishing, tennis and basketball courts, and trails for running, biking and horseback riding. But it's even better in the winter, serving as the perfect spot for snowmobiling, skiing and sledding.

AUGUST A. BUSCH MEMORIAL CONSERVATION AREA
St. Charles

2360 Hwy. D
St. Charles County, MO 63304
636.441.4554
www.mdc.mo.gov/regions/st-louis/august-busch-memorial-conservation-area
This is the ideal spot for families wanting to get out in the fresh air and interact with nature. Fishing, hiking, bird watching and hunting are just a few of the available options. Don't be surprised to come across everything from deer to turkey to beavers to owls. It also might be fun to take your son or daughter to the shooting and archery ranges and see what kind of a shot they are.

FOUNTAIN LAKES PARK
St. Charles

3850 Huster Rd.
St. Charles, MO 63301

Fountain Lakes Park offers lots of opportunities to catch glimpses of local wildlife and also includes 4 fishing lakes, paved trails that circle the lakes and a skate park for skateboarding and inline skating.

INDIAN CAMP CREEK PARK
St. Charles

1825 Dietrich Rd.
St. Charles, MO 63348-2635
www.parks.sccmo.org

Indian Camp Creek is the largest park in St. Charles, and one of the most unique. It features paved and natural trails, an eco-playground, a fishing lake and an observation tower that provides a spectacular view of the surrounding area housed in what used to be a grain silo.

LEWIS & CLARK BOAT HOUSE & NATURE CENTER
St. Charles

1050 S. Riverside Dr.
St. Charles, MO 63301
636.947.3199 | www.lewisandclark.net

Grab a bite at one of the excellent restaurants in historic St. Charles and then spend some time at this educational facility featuring exhibits relating to Lewis and Clark's famous expedition. Follow it up with a stroll down the St. Charles riverfront or come in May for Lewis and Clark Heritage Days.

YOUTH ACTIVITY PARK
St. Charles

7801 Hwy. N
Dardenne Prairie, MO 63368
636.561.4964 | www.parks.sccmo.org

A youth paradise, YAP boasts Missouri's largest skate park, an indoor recreation center, basketball and sand volleyball, rock climbing walls and more. If you can keep up with your kids here, more power to you. Membership is required.

ANTIQUE ROW
Soulard & Cherokee Street

Cherokee St.
St. Louis, MO 63118
www.cherokeeantiquerow.net

Window shopping can be fun if done in the right place. Take a stroll down Cherokee Antique Row, but don't let the name fool you—there's much more than just antiques to take in, and your family will get a kick out of the funky shops. Make the most of the experience by strolling west across Jefferson Avenue and grabbing a bite to eat at taco stand La Vallesana.

The Best Dad/Child Outdoor Parks & Recreation

BENTON PARK
Soulard & Cherokee Street
2200 Wyoming St.
St. Louis, MO 63118
www.bentonpark.com/content/benton-park
Amenities of this 14-acre park include a playground, horseshoe court, tennis courts, a stocked lake for fishing and a gorgeous reflecting pool. This is the perfect place to teach your kids about the grand St. Louis tradition that is the game of horseshoes.

LAFAYETTE PARK
Soulard & Cherokee Street
2101 Park Ave.
St. Louis, MO 63104
www.stlouis.missouri.org/citygov/parks/parks_div/lafayette.html
Old-time baseball contested under 19th century rules is played in the park on most Saturdays from spring to fall, making this a great day out for dads and their sons. Additionally, the gazebo can be rented out for picnics and special events.

LYON PARK
Soulard & Cherokee Street
S. Broadway and Arsenal St.
St Louis, MO 63118
Named after Civil War General Nathaniel Lyon and bearing a statue in his likeness, Lyon Park presents a great opportunity for dads and kids to grab a ball and bat and take advantage of the lighted softball fields.

SOULARD MARKET PARK
Soulard & Cherokee Street
Lafayette Ave. & S. 9th St.
St. Louis, MO 63104
Take a break from shopping at the Soulard Farmers Market and let the kids run around and play on the playground at Soulard Market Park.

CARONDELET PARK
South City
3700 Holly Hills Blvd.
St. Louis, MO 63116
www.stlouis.missouri.org/citygov/parks/parks_div/carondeletpark.html
A beautiful oasis in the heart of South City, Carondelet Park is home to stocked lakes perfect for fishing, softball and baseball fields, a boathouse and bandstand, horseshoe pits, playgrounds and more. On Sundays it's not uncommon to find a group of live action role players decked out and fighting with Nerf swords.

DOGTOWN STREET MUSICIANS FESTIVAL
South City

Tamm Ave. and Clayton Ave.
St Louis, MO 63139
www.twitter.com/DgtwnMusicFest

Presented in part by the Dogtown Historical Society, this annual outdoor festival celebrates the musical heritage of Dogtown by featuring local musicians playing up and down Tamm Ave. Awards are handed out at the conclusion of the festival, based on the decisions of the audience and a small panel of judges. This festival is a blast and all about music, food, fun and community.

FRANCIS PARK
South City

5300 Donovan Ave.
St. Louis, MO 63109
www.stlouis.missouri.org/citygov/parks/parks_div/Francis.html

A popular spot for tennis and handball players, there's also an awesome lily pad fountain and playground. In the summer there are free concerts by the Compton Heights Concert Bands every Saturday, and in the winter you can enjoy a Christmas tree lighting, free hot chocolate and cider, snacks, carriage rides and photos with Santa. The park is close to Ted Drewes frozen custard stand, which is a perfect way to cap off any day.

TILLES PARK
South City

Hampton and Fyler Aves.
St. Louis, MO 63139
www.stlouis.missouri.org/citygov/parks/parks_div/tilles.html

A popular neighborhood park, Tilles Park is ideal for getting out and stretching your legs if you're in the area. Stop by with some skates and take a spin around the roller hockey rink. This Tilles Park shouldn't be confused with the larger Mid County park of the same name.

TOWER GROVE PARK
South City

4256 Magnolia Ave.
St. Louis, MO 63110
314.771.2679 | www.towergrovepark.org

Come take advantage of walking trails, picnicking spots, sports fields, baseball diamonds, festivals in spring and fall, and gorgeous ponds. For a special treat, arrange for a horse-drawn carriage ride around the park or go on a Sunday afternoon and enjoy the brunch buffet offered inside Café Madeleine.

The Best Dad/Child Outdoor Parks & Recreation

BUDER PARK
South County

1919 Valley Park Rd.
Fenton, MO 63026
www.stlouisco.com/parks/buder.html

Buder Park features lots of peaceful, open space and is a local favorite due to its free archery range and huge air field where you can fly remote control planes and helicopters. As much fun as it is to watch the planes take flight, it's even more fun to get everything you need at Checkered Flag Hobby Country and join in the fun.

LAUMEIER SCULPTURE PARK
South County

12580 Rott Rd.
St. Louis, MO 63127
314.615.5278 | www.laumeier.org

A unique St. Louis experience, Laumeier Sculpture Park has been captivating visitors since its opening in 1977. Pack a picnic lunch and find a peaceful place to sit and appreciate the stunning contemporary sculptures of this open air museum, or inquire about one of their many special events, including the nationally acclaimed annual Art Fair.

STUCKMEYERS FARM MARKET AND GREENHOUSE
South County

249 Schneider Dr.
Fenton, MO 63026
636.349.1225 | www.stuckmeyers.com

A family owned vegetable farm that includes a pumpkin patch and "Fort Spooky" throughout September and October. Kids will also enjoy interacting with farm animals and hayrides. They also offer a special event in May where kids can decorate a free pot with free plant to bring home to mom for Mother's Day.

SUSON PARK
South County

6059 Wells Rd.
St. Louis, MO 63128
www.stlouisco.com/parks/suson.html

Suson Park offers a chance for families to experience country living. Kids can fish in the stocked ponds, one of which is reserved just for them, and walk through the horse and cow barns. Also represented are chickens, ducks, pigs and goats. There's a playground and multiple pavilions, so bring a lunch and plan on spending the day. Admission is free.

ULYSSES S. GRANT NATIONAL HISTORIC SITE
South County
7400 Grant Rd.
St. Louis, MO 63123
314.842.3298 | www.nps.gov/ulsg
Learn about 19th Century American life by touring Civil War general Ulysses S. Grant's historic home, White Haven. The surrounding grounds include many historic structures, and the park is home to various animals including bats and coyotes. Admission is free.

JANET MAJERUS PARK
University City
1300 Partridge Ave.
University City, MO 63130
www.ucityparksfoundation.org/ourparks/janetmajeruspark.html
Take a walk, join your kids in playing on the playground, relax by the pond or take advantage of the jogging trail and exercise stations.

KAUFMAN PARK
University City
999 Blackberry Pl.
St. Louis, MO 63130
Not far from the Delmar Loop, Kaufman Park features a beautiful wooded area, tennis courts, playground and "tot lot" play area for younger kids. On a fall day, plan a stop prior to a trip to nearby Your Pot's Desire.

RUTH PARK JUNIOR GOLF PROGRAM
University City
8211 Groby Rd.
University City, MO 63130
314.727.4800 | www.ucitymo.org/index.aspx?nid=505
The beautiful Ruth Park golf course in University City offers this summer golf program to kids ages 7 and up residing in University City and the surrounding areas. In addition to the camp, there are specific play days scheduled for parents and children.

ST. LOUIS WALK OF FAME
University City
6504 Delmar Blvd.
St. Louis, MO 63130-4501
314.727.7827 | www.stlouiswalkoffame.org
There's no need to travel all the way to Hollywood when you can stroll through the Delmar Loop, where the sidewalks are adorned with inlaid stars honoring the best and brightest of the many extraordinary folks associated with St. Louis. Kick off the walking tour with a trip to Blueberry Hill or Fitz's Rootbeer for lunch and wrap up with Fro Yo for dessert.

The Best Dad/Child Outdoor Parks & Recreation

UNIVERSITY CITY DOG PARK
University City

6860 Vernon Ave.
University City, MO 63130
314.505.8544
www.facebook.com/pages/U-City-Dog-Park/272002433183?v=info
Bring your kids and their puppy to this off-the-leash dog park and watch them both enjoy the freedom of running and playing in the fresh air. The park is fenced off, with a separate area for large dogs. Dogs must be registered and a liability form signed, and an annual fee is required; dogs must have proof of rabies vaccination.

CREVE COEUR PARK
West County

2143 Creve Coeur Mill Rd.
St. Louis, MO 63146
www.stlouisco.com/parks/creve.html
Creve Coeur Park provides a wonderful way to spend a spring or summer day. The park includes playgrounds, trails, tennis courts, a spray fountain, a disc golf course and archery range, fishing and sailing on the 320 acre lake. Swimming is not allowed, but kids will love the strip of sandy beach along the northeast shore.

GREENSFELDER EQUESTRIAN
West County

4250 Allenton Rd.
Wildwood, MO 63069-3145
636.458.1353 | www.greensfelderequestrian.com
Quality horseback riding lessons at reasonable rates are offered in the heart of beautiful Greensfelder Park in the rolling Ozark hills. Father/child lesson specials are available, so saddle up together and you'll be trotting around the ring in no time. Keep your eyes peeled on the drive out of the park and don't be surprised if you see a deer or two grazing along the side of the road.

LONE ELK PARK
West County

1 Lone Elk Park Rd.
St. Louis, MO 63088
www.stlouisco.com/parks/loneelk.html
Take a driving tour and enjoy seeing bison, deer, elk and waterfowl up close. There are many places throughout the park to get out of the car and enjoy a picnic lunch, and the World Bird Sanctuary is nearby. Admission to the park is free.

QUEENY PARK
West County

1599 S. Mason Rd.
St. Louis, MO 63131
www.stlouisco.com/parks/queeny.html

This sprawling 564-acre park includes the Dog Museum, The Greensfelder Recreation Complex, trails, multiple fishing holes, tennis courts and a massive playground with standard playground offerings and also some nice extras, like tunnels to crawl through, climbing rocks and lots of sandy space to run around.

WINDING BROOK ESTATE LAVENDER FARM
West County

3 Winding Brook Estate Dr.
Eureka, MO 63025
636.575.5572 | www.lavender.windingbrookestate.com

A relaxing visit to this 11-year old farmhouse is a perfect opportunity for father/daughter bonding. Activities and amenities include tours, lunch, tea & pastries, dessert, classes and u-pick harvesting. Mom will love it when you bring her home a bouquet of fresh lavender.

THE BEST DAD/CHILD
SPORTING EVENTS

2011 NCAA DIVISION III WOMEN'S VOLLEYBALL CHAMPIONSHIP

Washington University Field House
330 N. Big Bend Blvd.
St. Louis, MO 63130
314.935.5220 | www.ncaa.com/sports/volleyball-women/d3
November

Dads and daughters can cheer on the NCAA Division III women as they vie for the Volleyball Championship.

2011 NCAA MEN'S ICE HOCKEY WEST REGIONAL

Scottrade Center
1401 Clark Ave.
St. Louis, MO 63103
314.622.5435 | www.scottradecenter.com
March

The road to the NCAA "Frozen Four" skates through St. Louis. This is a great opportunity to see college hockey at its most competitive.

ARCH RIVAL ROLLER GIRLS

All American Sports Mall
11133 Lindbergh Business Ct.
St. Louis, MO 63123-7810
314.487.4625 | www.archrivalrollergirls.com
November through July

The Arch Rival Roller Girls are St. Louis's only all-female roller derby league. The league is made up of four teams: The M-80s, The Rebel Skate Alliance, The Smashinistas and The Stunt Devils. Dads are encouraged to bring their sons and daughters out to check out this sport that's rapidly growing in popularity.

BACKDRAFT RODEO

Lions Park
400 Bald Hill Rd.
Eureka, MO 63025
www.efpd.org/?mdp=rodeo

This annual rodeo, held in October, benefits the Fellowship of Eureka Firefighters. Kids will love the rodeo clown and talented riders as they take part in events ranging from cattle roping and barrel racing to bull riding.

The Best Dad/Child Sporting Events

GATEWAY GRIZZLIES

GCS Ballpark
2301 Grizzlie Bear Blvd.
Sauget, IL 62206
618.337.3000 | www.gatewaygrizzlies.com
May through September

The Gateway Grizzlies baseball team, affiliated with the Frontier League, is a treat for families, featuring fun and competitive baseball and a host of other attractions to complete the experience. Every Sunday is a Family Fun day where kids get the opportunity to run the bases, and there are always other fun events designed to entertain between innings. GCS Stadium is famous for its Krispy Kreme burger, a bacon cheeseburger served between a sliced Krispy Kreme doughnut.

MISSOURI VALLEY CONFERENCE MEN'S BASKETBALL TOURNAMENT

Scottrade Center
1401 Clark Ave.
St. Louis, MO 63103
314.622.5435 | www.mvc.org/archmadness
March

Come downtown to the Scottrade Center and be a part of March Madness. This is the nation's second longest running conference tournament and one of the best college basketball tournaments you'll ever see.

MISSOURI VALLEY CONFERENCE WOMEN'S BASKETBALL TOURNAMENT

The Family Arena
2002 Arena Pkwy.
St. Charles, MO 63303
636.896.4200 | www.mvc-sports.com
March

The ladies of the Missouri Valley Conference compete at the Family Arena in St. Charles, promising a thrilling tournament to crown the women's championship team. This would be a perfect day out for dads and daughters.

RIVER CITY RASCALS
900 T.R. Hughes Blvd.
O'Fallon, MO 63366
636.240.BATS | www.rivercityrascals.com
May through September
The River City Rascals, members of the Frontier league, is a baseball team specializing in competitive play and fun for all ages. The team's mascots like to roam the stands making friends and signing autographs, and the entertainment and promotions between innings are second to none. Their home stadium, T.R. Hughes Ballparks, includes a playground and other fun activity centers to keep kids active and entertained.

ST. LOUIS ACES
Dwight Davis Tennis Center
5620 Grand Dr.
St. Louis, MO 63112
314.361.0177 | www.stlouisaces.com
July
The St. Louis Aces offer the best in professional tennis, with a team consisting of top-ranked pros and special world renowned "Marquee Players" that have included Anna Kournikova, Pete Sampras and Serena Williams in past seasons. Aces events are designed to be fun, high-energy affairs and nothing fires up these athletes like an enthusiastic crowd.

ST. LOUIS BANDITS
16851 N. Outer 40
Chesterfield, MO 63005
636.536.4882 | www.stlouisbandits.pointstreaksites.com
September through March
The St. Louis Bandits is a Tier II Junior A ice hockey team in the North American Hockey League's North division and a treat for St. Louis hockey fans. Family nights include activities that kids will love, including face painting and prize giveaways.

ST. LOUIS BLUES
Scottrade Center
1401 Clark Ave.
St. Louis, MO 63103
314.622.5435 | www.blues.nhl.com
October through April
St. Louis hockey fans are some of the most rabid in the nation, and there's nothing better than taking in a home game and basking in the thrill and excitement of a Blues victory. Membership in the Jr. Blues Kids Club includes free tickets and additional tickets available at a discounted price, lots of cool memorabilia and the opportunity to shoot on the ice after a Jr. Bluenote game.

The Best Dad/Child Sporting Events

ST. LOUIS CARDINALS
Busch Stadium
700 Clark St.
St. Louis, MO 63102
314.345.9600 | www.stlouis.cardinals.mlb.com
April through October
St. Louis is first and foremost a baseball town, and nothing beats a night at Busch Stadium cheering on Major League Baseball's St. Louis Cardinals and laughing at the antics of Fredbird, the team's mascot. Busch Stadium contains many attractions for kids, including a Build-a-Bear station and a Family Pavilion that includes a batting cage and speed pitch game.

ST. LOUIS JR. BLUES
Affton Athletic Association
10300 Gravois Rd.
St. Louis, MO 63123
www.stlouisjrblues.pointstreaksites.com
September through March
The champion-caliber St. Louis Jr. Blues is part of the North American 3 Hockey League (NA3HL), and many of its members have gone on to illustrious college and professional careers. Catch an event to get a chance to see tomorrow's hockey stars today. Children's tickets are free.

ST. LOUIS RAMS
Edward Jones Dome
901 N. Broadway
St. Louis, MO 63101
314.342.5201 | www.stlouisrams.com
September through January
With a rookie quarterback poised to emerge as one of football's brightest stars in Sam Bradford, the St. Louis Rams are looking forward to taking the fight to opposing teams in upcoming seasons. Fortunately, families don't have to worry about braving the cold St. Louis weather to enjoy a game, thanks to the indoor Edward Jones Dome. Field Goal level Membership in the Rams Kids Club is free and includes a welcome letter from the coach and exclusive offers and invitations.

ST. LOUIS UNIVERSITY BILLIKENS
3330 Laclede Ave.
St. Louis, MO 63103
314.977.3177 | www.slubillikens.com
The SLU Billikens play all major college sports excluding football, with their basketball program having long been the talk of the town and their soccer team popular both on campus and off. Youth tickets are discounted for many events, including men's and women's soccer matches, and gameday promotions often consist of theme nights and giveaways.

UNIVERSITY OF MISSOURI ST. LOUIS TRITONS

225 Mark Twain Building, 1 University Blvd.
St. Louis, MO 63121
314.516.5661 | www.umsltritons.com

Formerly known as the Rivermen and Riverwomen, the newly branded UMSL Tritons participate in all major college sports except football. There is no charge for admission to baseball and softball games, and tickets for children under 6 years old are free to men's and women's basketball and soccer events and women's volleyball games.

THE BEST DAD/CHILD
UNIQUE ADVENTURES

AMTRAK RIVER RUNNER
110 West Argonne Dr.
Kirkwood, MO 63122
800.USA.RAIL | www.amtrak.com
Travel Time: Approximately 6 hours each way
Costs: Approximately $40 per ticket

No doubt your child has gotten interested in toy trains thanks to the many specialty shops in the St. Louis area that offer wooden and metal trains and train sets. Why not take things to the next level and treat them to the real thing? Depart from historic downtown Kirkwood in Mid County and take the River Runner route to Kansas City. Thanks to the Trails & Rails program, a guide from the National Parks Service will be onboard to offer insight and information along the way. Spend the night exploring Kansas City or just make a day of it. Be forewarned—the trains do their best, but they don't always run on time.

CHESTERFIELD ARTS
444 Chesterfield Ctr.
Chesterfield, MO 63017
636.519.1955 | www.chesterfieldarts.org
Travel Time: Half an hour drive from Downtown St. Louis
Costs: Free

Chesterfield Arts presents visual, performing, literary and outdoor art that's guaranteed to impress the artist in your family (and even the non-artists, as well). Featuring special events and rotating exhibits for the whole family, you're sure to find something cool at Chesterfield Arts. Speaking of cool, make sure you check out The Awakening – Buried Giant, which is exactly what it sounds like: a sculpture of a buried giant waking up and breaking through the ground. This second casting of the sculpture will provide the backdrop for an awesome photo-op and a great memory. Go ahead and climb into the giant's hand or take a seat on his big toe.

BENDER STATUE ROAD TRIP
7728 Hwy. 30
Dittmer, MO 63023-1816
636.285.2122
Travel Time: An hour drive from Downtown St. Louis
Costs: Hotel rates vary by season

Taking a road trip to an auto repair shop in rural Dittmer, MO may not seem like the likely backdrop for adventure. But it is when that the trip features a one-of-a-kind giant statue of the robot Bender from the television show Futurama made out of junk. After seeing the statue, head back to Pacific, where you can follow historic route 66 up to Eureka. Make a night of it by staying in the Holiday Inn near Six Flags amusement park; the heated indoor pool and arcade/game area are every kid's dream. Go off season to get a break from the "winter blahs" and reduced rates.

The Best Dad/Child Unique Adventures

CAHOKIA MOUNDS
30 Ramey St.
Collinsville, IL 62234
618.346.5160 | www.cahokiamounds.org
Travel Time: 15 minutes drive from Downtown St. Louis
Costs: Free but donation of $10 for families is suggested
Explore the artfully preserved remains of the only prehistoric native civilization north of Mexico at this archeological site, the largest in America. Spend some time taking in the exhibits in the Interpretive Center and then head outside to conquer Monks Mound, the largest of the impressive mounds at 92 feet high and 951 feet long. See who can win a race to the top, but watch your step.

THE CAVE RESTAURANT AND RESORT
26880 Rochester Rd.
Richland, MO 65556
573.765.4554 | www.thecaverestaurantandresort.com
Travel Time: Approx. 2.5 hours drive from Downtown St. Louis
Costs: Vary, with special discounted packages available
For your next camping trip, consider The Cave Restaurant and Resort. Bring a tent or rent a furnished cabin for the night, but be sure to get up early to enjoy the beautiful sunrise as you head out to the Gasconade River for canoeing or fishing. After spending the day floating down the river, grab dinner at the only restaurant in the United States located inside a cave. That's right, a real cave, complete with waterfalls.

THE EDGE
701 S. Belt West
Belleville, IL 62220-2415
618.236.2101 | www.edgefun.net
Travel Time: Half an hour drive from Downtown St. Louis
Costs: Varies by activity
Prove to your kids and their friends that you're the coolest dad ever by loading up the car and making the drive across the river to The Edge in Belleville, IL. Start off with a round of laser tag in the world's largest laser tag arena, a sprawling neon fantasy world with plenty of places to run and hide while your kids try to tag you with their lasers. Take a break and grab a bite to eat at the snack bar or d.s. vespers, the full service, family-friendly restaurant located in the same building, and then finish up the day with a round of mini golf and some quality arcade time.

GEOCACHING

Numerous locations throughout St. Louis and Missouri
www.geocaching.com
Travel Time: Varies
Costs: Free

Geocaching offers all of the excitement of a treasure hunt with none of the inherent risks (angry pirates, quicksand, traitorous partners, etc.). All you need is a GPS or Geocaching app for your iPhone or Android and you'll be ready to go. Find GPS coordinates online and follow the path to hidden treasure. Just be sure that you bring something to replace the treasure with; that's part of the fun. Geocaching can be a fun way to spend an afternoon or an entire weekend, depending on the scope of your treasure hunt. Find geocaches at www.geocaching.com.

JBARH BISON RANCH

10802 Sunnyside School Rd.
Trenton, IL 62293
618.934.3029 | www.jbarhbisonranch.com
Travel time: Approximately one hour drive from Downtown St. Louis
Costs: Vary, approximately $20 to 30 for adults and $10 to 20 for children; kids under 3 are free.

Come meet the herd of sociable bison that roam the fields of the JbarH Bison Ranch and enjoy a tour of the working ranch. Watch out for Paco, an 800 lb. bison with a sweet tooth and a preference for Twinkies and make sure you bring a camera to take pictures of the kids petting the baby bison. In addition to bisons, you'll also encounter alpacas, horses and Sadie, a Sicilian donkey.

LITTLE DIXIE CONSERVATION AREA

1821 State Road RA
Fulton, MO 65251
573.884.6861
Travel Time: Approximately 2 hours drive from Downtown St. Louis
Costs: Admission is free; row boat rental is $5/day, April through October

Pack a lunch and spend a summer day in the great outdoors at Little Dixie and enjoy all that this quiet conservation area has to offer, including Little Dixie Lake; you can bring your own boat or rent a row boat for the day, but be sure to bring sunscreen and life vests as only boat and oars are provided. Once back on dry land, take a hike through the dense oak-hickory forest surrounding the lake and pause long enough to enjoy your picnic lunch. The little ones are sure to be worn out on the drive home thanks to all the fresh air.

The Best Dad/Child Unique Adventures

MASTODON STATE HISTORIC SITE
1050 Charles J. Becker Dr.
Imperial, MO 63052
636.464.2976 | www.mostateparks.com/mastodon.htm
Travel time: Approximately 30 minute drive from Downtown St. Louis
Costs: Museum fee is $4 for adults, kids admitted free
Your son will get excited when you use the words "mastodon" and "bone bed" in describing what the day holds in store. Mastodon State Historic site is home to the Kimmswick Bone Bed, where the bones of mastodons and other extinct animals were found in the 1800s. Visit the museum and marvel at the full-size replica of a mastodon skeleton and hike the Wildflower Trail out to the Bone Bed; Fossil Day is in June and gives families the chance to hunt for fossils.

MERAMEC CAVERNS
Stanton, MO
573.468.CAVE | www.americascave.com
Travel time: Approximately 1.5 hours drive from Downtown St. Louis
Costs: Cave admission is $19.00 for Adults, $9.50 for kids ages 5-11, kids 4 and under free. Other fees apply for additional activities.
Cave tours are offered daily throughout Meramec Caverns, the one-time hideout of outlaw Jesse James and home of some of the largest and rarest cave formations in the world. Augment the adventure with turns on the zip line that crosses the Meramec River, a riverboat ride or a canoe float trip.

NATIONAL GREAT RIVERS MUSEUM
#2 Locks & Dam Way
Alton, IL 62002
877.462.6979
www.mvs.usace.army.mil/Recreation/RiversProject/museum.html
Travel Time: Approximately 40 minutes drive from Downtown St. Louis
Cost: General admission is free, some activities may require fees
It's nice to find an adventure that's both fun and educational, and the National Great Rivers Museum and related activities excels on both counts. Learn about the significance of the Mississippi River at the museum and then spend the day taking advantage of your favorite outdoor recreation activities at the various areas around the Mississippi. Some choices include biking, kayaking, bird watching, hunting or even gliding along the levee on a rented Segway.

PURINA FARMS

200 Checkerboard Dr.
Gray Summit, MO 63039
314.982.3232 | www.purina.com
Travel Time: Approximately 1 hour drive from Downtown St. Louis
Costs: General admission to Visitor's Center is free

Lots of attractions await your family at Purina Farms, chief among them the Barn and Play Area, which includes a variety of animals typically found on a farm. Kids can milk a cow and pet baby animals in the nursery before climbing into the barn's hayloft and swinging from a rope. Other animals on display include cows, horses, chickens and herding dogs, who love to perform for an audience. Purina's Pet Center is home to many dogs and cats and a 20-ft.-tall cat house.

ST. LOUIS RAMS TRAINING CAMP

Russell Training Center
One Rams Way
Earth City, MO 63045
314.516.8852
www.stlouisrams.com/news-and-events/training-camp.html
Travel Time: Approximately 30 minute drive from Downtown St. Louis
Costs: Free

Get up close and personal with the St. Louis Rams as they prepare for the upcoming season. Prior to the start of the NFL season in September, the St. Louis Rams hold a series of practices open to the public, usually concluding with a scrimmage held at Lindenwood University in St. Charles. These practices are a great chance for your kids to get autographs from their favorite players.

SHAW NATURE RESERVE

Hwy. 100 & I-44
Gray Summit, MO 63039
636.451.3512 | www.shawnature.org
Travel Time: 45 minute drive from Downtown St. Louis
Costs: General admission is $3 for adults, free for kids 12 and under

Lace up your most comfortable hiking boots and explore the many hiking trails available at Shaw Nature Reserve. Plan your visit in the spring and bring a camera so you can get pictures of the various trees, flowers and native plants in full bloom. Enjoy strolling on the boardwalk over the wetlands, or bring mom on Mother's Day weekend to the Spring Wildflower Sale; be sure to check out the other special events held throughout the year.

ABOUT THE AUTHOR

Adam Bodendieck is a freelance writer who lives near St. Louis, Missouri with his wife and 3 kids. When he's not writing, he's playing with one of the family's many pets, which include cats, dogs, a horse and an alpaca. He's hoping to add chickens and goats to that list soon. More than anything else, he strives to be a WonderDad and a WonderHusband.

THANK YOUS

Thank you to Dylan, Blake and Christopher for being such WonderKids, and to Heather for being the world's greatest WonderMom. You're the inspiration for this book and I look forward to all of the great adventures we're going to have. A special thanks to my family and friends for all of their ideas and suggestions.